THE

Home Flipper's

JOURNAL

THE

Home Flipper's

JOURNAL

Your All-in-One Logbook for Organizing
and Executing a Successful Home Flip

NANCY DUNHAM

ULYSSES
PRESS

Published in the United States by:
Ulysses Press
PO Box 3440
Berkeley, CA 94703
www.ulyssespress.com

ISBN: 978-1-64604-198-5
Library of Congress Control Number: 2021931515

Printed in the United States by Kingery Printing Company
10 9 8 7 6 5 4 3 2 1

Acquisitions editor: Ashten Evans
Managing editor: Claire Chun
Project manager: Bridget Thoreson
Editor: Renee Rutledge
Proofreader: Barbara Schultz
Front cover design: Hejab Malik
Interior design and layout: what!design @ whatweb.com
Artwork: page 5 emoji © stas11/shutterstock.com

For Wayne

Contents

Worksheet Appendix 90

Introduction

It's difficult to hear home-flipping success stories and not want to dive into an undertaking of your own. Home-flipping experts on television and online seem to easily convert a house, have fun doing it, and walk away with a significant profit. What's not to love?

What the gurus don't tell you, though, is that to make a profit, you must plan, invest time and money, and, let's face it, have a bit of luck. If those stars align, you can succeed at home flipping. But don't expect to make money right away. If you're fortunate on your first few projects, you'll break even. You need to learn the ropes before you can hope to earn money. And then, don't expect more than about 20 percent *net* profit.

I can't promise you luck, but if you follow the guidelines in this book and plan your project, you may just create your good fortune.

What Type of Home Flipper Are You?

My late husband and I flipped a few homes in the Washington, DC, area, and my parents also flipped a home in upstate New York. All the projects were entirely different types of properties, including an old barn, a detached house, and an urban townhome. All had completely different areas that needed to be shored up. And, finally, all took different amounts of time.

That brings up one of the first points you should know. The phrase "home flipping" is a catchall term that has become somewhat generic over the years. The difference between your "home flipping" and ours likely comes down to goals.

In general, there are three main types of home flipping.

TYPE 1. For the first type of home flipping, you buy a bargain home in a hot or up-and-coming real estate market, do no or minimal repairs and upgrades, hold onto the residence until the market price significantly increases, and then resell the property for a profit. Many people who flip properties in this way often lease them to others until they think the market or their circumstance indicates it's an excellent time to sell.

I currently live in Austin, Texas, and there are many such home flippers here, especially in the ultra-hot downtown area. A significant number buy condos in modern, high-demand high-rises. The investors do minimal repairs (there are exceptions where they go all out by tearing down walls and creating state-of-the-art chef's kitchens, of course). Then they either sell the property as soon as possible or rent the home and only sell when the market is ripe.

> **CAUTION:** Check zoning laws in the area and neighborhoods in which you want to buy. Many do not allow vacation rentals in specific neighborhoods or subdivisions. Also, be aware that some homeowners' associations (HOAs) and other governing entities have even more rules about what you can and cannot do to a property. That can go as far as painting the outside of the home. In fact, some HOAs require the owner to use the property as their primary residence for a certain amount of time (usually one or two years) before they can lease it to someone else. Other HOAs only allow a tiny percentage of owners to rent out their homes as investments. The reason is that it is more difficult to sell a home in a neighborhood where many houses are rentals.

TYPE 2. Another type of home flipping entails buying a home in up-and-coming or already-desirable neighborhoods. Often, these homes are foreclosures or sold as part of an estate. These investors rip the house down to the studs or completely demolish the home and rebuild it.

These home flippers almost always need stable finances and a team of contractors—painters, contractors, and landscapers—behind them to make the venture viable. My parents flipped a house this way with minimal outside labor. It was a costly and failed venture.

TYPE 3. This book is written primarily for the third type of home flipper. (Yes, we arguably saved the best for last!) These investors buy a home, renovate, repair, and update it, and then resell it right away for a profit.

Whatever your renovation plan, you've come to the right place! Whether you are interested in one of the home-flipping projects outlined above or even a hybrid project such as the one my husband and I undertook, this book is full of guidance, advice, and tools that will save you plenty of time, effort, and money.

That's important because you never know if the residence you flip will become a project of such love that you opt to live there.

That happened to me. My late husband and I bought a DC area property to flip for resale. Once we started renovating, we fell so in love with it that we ended up moving in ourselves!

Yes, we made a significant profit when we sold that house, but with perfect 20/20 hindsight, I can see several missteps we made that cost us time, money, and labor.

Sharing the Knowledge

Much of my 20/20 hindsight comes from personal experience, but even more is from hundreds of realtors, contractors, home inspectors, insurance agents, and home flippers I spoke with during my 20-plus years of writing and editing stories about real estate, home flipping, and home improvement for major news media outlets. In many cases, the articles I wrote were only the catalyst that ignited my exploration of both the upsides and stumbling blocks of home flipping. Whatever your goal, you'll find tips in each chapter to guide you toward solutions and resources if your project takes an unexpected turn.

In addition to advice stemming from my own experiences, I've included quotes and tidbits from many of the industry professionals I met and interviewed. After all, nothing beats guidance from expert home flippers or those who work with them every day. That's because each choice you make—whether it involves tearing down a wall or replacing a lighting fixture—can impact every other part of your project.

Of course, all the advice in the world isn't helpful if you aren't organized. That's why I designed this book for you to use as a one-stop companion. In addition to offering time-tested guidance, it's also a journal and organizer where you can sketch out ideas; track options, choices, and inventory items; track expenses; log information about trade and real estate professionals; and even inspire how you'll design the all-important curb appeal.

Before we start, it's essential to understand what this book is not. It's not full of ways to get rich quickly. It's not a source to tell you how much, where, or when to invest in real estate. It doesn't explain pricing strategies. And it's certainly not a guarantee that the place you flip will sell for the price you want.

This journal is a step-by-step guide about what to consider as you approach a house-flipping project. It's filled with practical, step-by-step advice.

My goal in writing this book is to give you an honest breakdown of what you need to know and do to move toward a successful flip. Consider this guide as you work to transform your chosen property into a flipped jewel and move toward selling it for a profit.

CHAPTER 1

What Is Home Flipping?

"Hi, Nancy 😀 . I just tried to call you...are you looking for a home to live in—or are you an investor looking for a fix and flip or rent?—this is [name withheld] of [real estate firm withheld]."

That's a text message I received when I began to house hunt in Austin, Texas. I mention this because you'll likely receive such texts when you start online searches for investment properties you hope to renovate and resell.

Why not search online, right? It's fun to see what's out there. As long as you just browse, you are fine. It's when you take the next step that you may stumble into financial quicksand.

> **CAUTION:** You're not ready to talk to a realtor or any other property seller yet. Don't even go "just to look." It's too easy to get caught up in the excitement and make a costly buying mistake.

Sure, you may find a property that works well as a rehab, but many more elements are involved in choosing a property that will make a successful flip.

> **CAUTION:** Don't think that because you've bought and sold homes for your primary residence, you can skip all the reading, planning, and budgeting outlined in this book. That's not true. Buying a property for resale is not about your personal tastes, lifestyle, or even your budget. It's about maximizing your investment.

If you're serious about buying and flipping a property for profit, you owe it to yourself to boost your knowledge of real estate, home flipping, finance, and many other topics. No, studying these topics isn't as much fun as shopping for or even planning a home's renovation. If you want to succeed as a home flipper, though, you need to put in the time to learn the fundamentals. Beyond that, you need to remember this is an investment, not a personal dream project.

"The most important part of the whole equation is really knowing your numbers at the beginning," says home investor and realtor Marcia Castro-Socas of Orlando. "You have to be able to estimate how much you should put into the project based on how much you're going to be able to sell it for a year from now. That takes some knowledge."

Castro-Socas says many investors, even some savvy ones, are caught holding investment properties when the market implodes. That can lead ill-prepared investors into financial straits.

"Before you buy and as you go along, educate yourself as much as possible," she says. "There are a lot of free resources you can use to get started. I don't recommend people spend money on educational trainers in the beginning. You've just got to learn the basics first."

A Word about the Term "Flipped Home"

Most people think of the term "flipped home" in one way—basically, as an investment property, usually for the purpose of some form of renovation and then resale or rental until it is sold.

In some circles, the term "flipped home" is pejorative. That's because some less-than-scrupulous people have adopted the term. In those cases, the term can be synonymous with "a shady or poor quality" renovation.

Clearly, *you* won't do a shoddy type of renovation. And you don't want others to think the home you flipped is anything but a well-renovated jewel. That's why it's best to use the term "home renovation" when talking to realtors, contractors, and even acquaintances.

Renovations before and after the COVID-19 Pandemic

According to the National Association of Home Builders (NAHB), kitchen and bathroom remodels were the top improvements before the pandemic. Although those renovations continued to be popular, renovating decks, patios, and porches, and updating landscaping also flourished. It's no secret that the pandemic ushered in a rush of all types of home improvement projects.

At the beginning of the pandemic in March and April 2020, the market for home remodeling dipped significantly, according to NAHB. That market recovered by February 2021.

"NAHB estimates that real spending on home improvements will continue to increase in 2021 and 2022 throughout the COVID-19 pandemic," says Paul Emrath, PhD, NAHB's assistant vice president for surveys and housing policy research. "The biggest factors prohibiting stronger growth are mainly the volatile material prices and labor shortages."

So you'll feel the pinch of those shortages. Perhaps one plus, though, is that early 2021 brought record lumber prices that forced the delay of some new housing projects and caused some buyers to back out of sales, creating more inventory for potential buyers.

The Market for Flipped Homes

When you sell something, it's always a great idea to understand the overall market for it. Take the current COVID-19 pandemic. The good news for homebuyers is that social distancing and other cultural shifts have decreased the number of real estate investors and increased the number of first-time buyers.

The National Association of Realtors (NAR) reports that first-time homebuyers accounted for 31 percent of all homes purchased between June 2019 and June 2020, consistent with the same period of the previous year. NAR reported 81 percent of those homes were detached, single-family homes. Of the homes built, 9 percent of buyers had one or more investment properties.

What does that mean to you? As of this writing, you'll likely have a better selection of homes in hot areas that some long-time investors might have snapped up a year or two ago. Your best bet to make a profit is to buy a home, renovate it, and then rent it until the market and economy are more robust. Flipping a house to resell it immediately might not be wise.

The Market Shifts, Sometimes Quickly

So why am I telling you this? I want you to know that the market has likely shifted—maybe dramatically—since NAR published the data I listed above. I'm also telling you this because you need to know what type of real estate climate you would enter before buying a property to renovate.

Plenty of sources will give you insights, but you want unbiased ones. Many realtors, financial advisors, and even news sources have financial stakes in the information they offer. Don't ignore them, but verify what they report.

You can find some reasonably unbiased advice at:

- **THE NATIONAL ASSOCIATION OF REALTORS**, www.nar.realtor. NAR is a membership of 1.4 million real estate industry professionals, including residential and commercial brokers, property managers, and appraisers. The website is an excellent resource for real estate education, research and statistics, and other real estate topics.

- **BIGGERPOCKETS**, BiggerPockets.com. This is a well-known chat board of investing enthusiasts. Many people who have successfully entered the home-flipping arena swear by BiggerPockets.

- **RAMSEY SOLUTIONS**, RamseySolutions.com. This is my favorite blog from financial expert Dave Ramsey. Ramsey's team fills the site with an array of real estate news, financial advice, renovation trends, and much more.

How Do I Know When or If I Should Buy?

There's no way to know with 100 percent certainty that you can buy a house, renovate it, and make a profit. When you hear that it's a buyer's market, that means that it's likely not a great time to sell a property. When you hear it's a seller's market, the reverse is true.

The best way to decide when to buy a home to flip is to plan. First of all, detail your goals. For example: I want the income from this property to pay the mortgage on it.

Write down your goals:

Next, calculate the maximum price of your property with the Do the Math to Meet Your Goal worksheet (see also page 91). The rule of thumb is never to pay more than 70 percent of the after repair value (ARV) of the house.

Do the Math to Meet Your Goal

	AMOUNT
1. Future sale of the house	
2. Divide the amount by 1.20 (for a 20 percent profit).	
3. Determine the cost of repairs and renovations.	
4. Analyze other costs: Real estate agent fees	
Closing costs	
Property taxes (6 months)	
HOA fees (6 months)	
5. Maximum price to pay for the house	

Once you know your goals and how much capital you have to work with, answer these questions:

1. How much time can I commit to this project? Be specific, like 10 hours a week or every Sunday.

2. Are there available properties?   Y / N

3. Is this a good time to get into the real estate market?   Y / N

Don't be daunted. You have this book that spells out the step-by-step plan to ensure you have the proper tools to make a smart financial decision for your specific circumstances.

How Much Money Will I Make?

As you likely know, there are no guarantees about how much money your flipped home will net you despite what reality shows lead you to believe. It depends on many factors, including some out of your control, such as market fluctuations, crime statistics, school ratings, employment opportunities, and more.

TIP: Many experts advise you not to expect to make a profit on the first, second, or even perhaps third property you flip. Those properties are learning experiences for you. Approach them as such. Of course, you don't want to lose your shirt either. We'll talk about how to avoid that in a bit. For now, though, realize that your first home-flipping projects are educational. Yes, you can make a decent profit. But don't count on it.

With that in mind, note that the average gross profit earned by someone who flipped a home in 2019 was $62,900 nationwide, according to ATTOM Data Solution, a national property database.

The key words in that statement are "gross profit." The sellers didn't walk away with $69,000. They may not have made any net profit once they paid for the home, renovations, and other expenses that people may not think about, including permits, debris disposal, closing costs, realtor commissions, and more.

That's why it's vital to ensure you buy low, use cost-effective strategies to rehab the property, and feel confident you can sell at a high price.

You can decide if you want to spend more money on a property or work on more renovations than we advise. Just know that you will literally pay if you go overboard on the purchase price of your investment home or any part of a renovation.

This book offers you a step-by-step guide to ensure the home you flip is truly an investment that will pay off for you in the long run.

Before You Jump In

Before you move ahead in this book and on your plan, there are some things you should consider. Home flipping is positive for many people, but definitely not for everyone. Keep these points in mind as you move ahead:

- **LIMIT OR AVOID TAKING ON EXCESSIVE DEBT.** Cash is king when you go into home flipping. There are different ways to obtain that cash (which we'll discuss later). The bottom line—you do not want to begin home flipping if you already have debt.

- **START SMALL.** When you begin home flipping, you likely don't want to tear a home down to the studs and rebuild. Look for a home that needs some paint, new doorknobs, new light switches, and other minor renovations.

"I would definitely say when it comes to the first property, keep things simple," advises Lucas Machado, president of House Heroes, a company that buys and flips houses in Sunny Isles Beach, Florida. "Don't do a massive renovation. Stick to something simple, cosmetic. In the current [2021] market, people are selling quickly, at retail, with just cleaning and doing minor renovations. For your first deal, do something cosmetic."

Stalling home building projects and a hot sellers' market make this a great time to invest in just such a property. But heed Machado's warning. Renovations making a big difference to prospective buyers include new doorknobs, modern light switches, and perhaps paint.

Financial guru Dave Ramsey says it more bluntly:

> *"Dreams of gleaming hardwood floors, on-trend light fixtures, and fabulous kitchens with professional-grade stoves can quickly cause your renovations to get out of hand... Don't forget that significant renovations—like kitchens and bathrooms—can easily make or break your flip."*

Take the kitchen, for example.

According to the 2020 Cost vs. Value Report, which compares average costs for remodeling projects and the value they retain at resale, the average amount spent on a major kitchen remodel is almost $68,500. The average amount regained from that cost is only around $40,000. That's not the kind of ROI (return on investment) you want to see when you're flipping a house.

While you might invest in a couple of major updates on a flip, don't underestimate the power of small tweaks. Things like a fresh coat of paint, updated hardware, and new landscaping can make a huge impact!"

- **EDUCATE YOURSELF.** I've mentioned a few sites (DaveRamsey.com and BiggerPockets.com) that offer smart advice for those who want to flip a home. Many investors say they didn't pay private mentors for education at first. Instead, soak up all the knowledge you can through well-respected websites, forums, podcasts, and, of course, talking to other investors. And, of course, find and speak with established realtors.

- **CONSIDER OBTAINING A REAL ESTATE LICENSE.** No, you might not want to do that right away, but it wouldn't be wrong to do so. You don't need a license to flip a house, of course. Having one does give you advantages, including knowing the ins and outs of contracts; access to the Multiple Listing Service (MLS), a real-time database of homes for sale throughout the United States; and knowledge of the best strategies to buy and sell successfully. Plus, you'll get to know some of the best (and worst!) contractors, home inspectors, and other real estate professionals in the business.

- PLAN FOR MANY EXIT STRATEGIES. You never know what might go wrong in any part of a flip. That's why it's vital to make sure you have exit strategies. There are various strategies for the many different stages of the home-flipping journey. One of the most popular might be renting rather than selling a property.

CHAPTER 2

Your Finances

If you're like many people, you want to try renovating a home and selling it, but you're not sure how to finance it. Do you try to take out a loan? Do you take a second mortgage out on your house? Do you dip into your savings?

Despite what the reality shows on television portray, the odds of buying, quickly flipping, and coming out with a high profit on your first flip, second flip, or any other subsequent flips are about the same as your chances of winning the lottery

"I am very conservative by nature," says investor Kyle McCormick of Hershey, Pennsylvania. "People think I am wheeling and dealing, throwing thousands of money [sic] around. They don't realize I spend a lot of time analyzing properties, getting outbid on properties, and that's okay. I often think, 'Whoever paid that much for the property is going to lose a lot of money.'"

McCormick credits a conservative approach for making a profit on 9 out of 10 properties.

> **TIP:** When you flip a home, the old saying "Hope for the best but expect the worst" is a wise motto. Yes, home flipping can be profitable. But you want to maintain objectivity and a business-like attitude so you can pull the rip cord on the home-flipping parachute and exit with as much of your money intact as possible.

Creating Your Budget

The first step to a successful home renovation is formulating a realistic budget. This means calculating the costs for any work you will need to do before selling the house. Organize the projects by general areas of the home:

- landscaping (resodding or reseeding the lawn, trimming the foliage, power washing the walkways)

- home exterior (painting, fixing the railings, replacing the siding)

- home interior (renovating the bathroom, resurfacing the hardwood floors)

I like to record the various projects in a form like this:

Estimated Repair Costs: Landscaping

Project:	Budget:
Details:	
Contractor:	Contact information:
Notes:	

Estimated Repair Costs: Home Exterior

Project: | Budget:

Details:

Contractor: | Contact information:

Notes:

Estimated Repair Costs: Home Interior

Project: | Budget:

Details:

Contractor: | Contact information:

Notes:

Estimated Repair Costs: Additional Projects

Project: | Budget:

Details:

Contractor: | Contact information:

Notes:

Use the Estimated Repair Costs worksheets starting on page 92 to track the costs of your repairs and renovations.

When you've finished filling out the Do the Math to Meet Your Goal form (page 10 or page 91) and Estimated Repair Costs worksheets, you can determine your overall costs with the Total Budget worksheet (see also page 108).

Total Budget

		AMOUNT
Estimated purchase price (see Do The Math to Meet Your Goal, page 10):		
Estimated fees (see Do The Math to Meet Your Goal, page 10):		
Estimated Repair Costs	Landscaping:	
	Home Exterior:	
	Home Interior:	
	Additional Projects:	
Total:		

Keep this standard in mind: If you truly want a chance to make money when you flip a home, it's vital to remember the 70 percent rule. That means you should never pay more than 70 percent of a home's ARV. So if you believe you could sell a property for $100,000 (after rehab), but it needs $20,000 in upgrades and renovations, you don't want to pay more than $56,000.

> **TIP:** If you opt to hire a realtor to help you with the sale, they can help you determine precisely what renovations will net you the highest return and what resale price you can expect. Of course, there are no guarantees, but realtors make their living making educated predictions about home values.

Financing a Home

Another critical step is to decide how—and even if—you can finance a home flip. Infomercials, reality shows, and advertisements all ballyhoo the easy loans that are available for most people. Many of those are akin to the "No Credit, Bad Credit" signs you see in front of some used car lots. The bottom line—home flipping is expensive, and you want to make sure doing one doesn't undermine your lifestyle. After all, you still have to pay the mortgage or rent on your residence, keep the utilities on, buy food, pay for transportation, and cover all of the other expenses of everyday living.

"I learned about investing by reading BiggerPockets and listening to their podcast," McCormick says. "Those are good for beginners. BiggerPockets absolutely helped me get started."

Here are some options to finance your flipped home:

1. Liquid savings

2. Refinancing primary home

3. Home equity loan

4. Home equity financing

5. Home equity line of credit

6. Reverse mortgage

7. Private money lenders

8. Traditional bank loan

9. Taking on other investors

10. Hard money lenders

This Financing Your Home worksheet on the following page and page 109 will help you determine what money you have available to purchase a house.

Financing Your Home

Liquid savings	Company:	Estimated amount:	Contact information:
	Notes:		
Refinancing primary home	Company:	Estimated amount:	Contact information:
	Notes:		
Home equity loan	Company:	Estimated amount:	Contact information:
	Notes:		
Home equity financing	Company:	Estimated amount:	Contact information:
	Notes:		
Home equity line of credit	Company:	Estimated amount:	Contact information:
	Notes:		
Reverse mortgage	Company:	Estimated amount:	Contact information:
	Notes:		
Private money lenders	Company:	Estimated amount:	Contact information:
	Notes:		
Traditional bank loan	Company:	Estimated amount:	Contact information:
	Notes:		
Taking on other investors	Company:	Estimated amount:	Contact information:
	Notes:		
Hard money lenders	Company:	Estimated amount:	Contact information:
	Notes:		

Case Study

Investor Erik Wright of Tennessee moved into home renovations full time about two years ago. He got into home flipping in a different way from the way many others do. He and his friends lived together in a large home owned by another friend. The owners' plans changed, and they were forced to move. That's when Wright decided to buy a home where he and his friends could live. In effect, he became the landlord. The rent they paid him more than covered the mortgage and renovations.

"At that time, I didn't know anything about house flipping. I didn't know anything about real estate investing," he says. "I just did it out of necessity."

Yet Wright didn't go into the investment blindly. He had a secure job, so he knew he could pay the mortgage, even if his friends opted out of the living arrangement. He renovated the house on his own and sold it three years later, netting a $15,000 profit after having "lived for free for three years."

At that time, Wright moved to a different city and found a duplex for sale. He says that was the point when he felt that home flipping was something he should seriously consider. Today he has multiple properties he bought and flipped. Almost all of them are rental properties that he pays property managers to oversee.

> *"And I always recommend that you go into a house knowing that you can afford to pay the mortgage on your own even if you don't have any tenants. And so that's what I did. I knew that I could make this $750-a-month mortgage without any payment because of the income from my job....and that's just kind of icing on the cake."*

That's just the type of plan financial guru Dave Ramsey recommends.

EXPERT ADVICE

Dave Ramsey

"Most importantly, doing any kind of 'investment' with debt is a dumb plan. Period," Ramsey writes on a Ramsey Solutions blog post. "Trying to sell a flipped house for more money than you invested in it is already a risk—even with cash. Using debt in the process skyrockets your chance of losing money if there's a hiccup in your plans."

Why Cash Is King

Whether you buy a home to flip or as your own residence, you want to pay in cash whenever possible. There are many reasons for that. Perhaps the most important one is that sellers prefer cash-paying customers. When home sellers receive offers that are contingent on financing, they may have to relist the home if the financing doesn't come through. Although many first-time investors may feel that paying in cash is not feasible, it's the best possible way to finance flips. It's worth the effort to make it work.

In addition, when traditional lenders finance homes, they generally want extra inspections and paperwork. This caveat does not mean you should skip a home inspection or property assessment when you buy a home with cash. It just means that the decision-maker is you. That allows you and the seller to negotiate without input from the bank or other lenders.

There are many ways to raise the amount of cash you need to buy a home. Arguably the easiest way is to sell another property. That's something I did when I changed residences. You may not have property or another major asset to flip. There are other ways to raise the money you need for the flip. Consider some of the most popular ones for first-time home flippers.

Consider Your Assets

What money do you have? Do you have investments that you can access from savings, savings bonds, or other accounts? Of course, home sellers won't take your word on the amount of cash you can access. Talk to your banker or other financial representative and ask them to provide a letter stating the dollar amount you can access. You can also work with that banker or representative to verify the amount you have in the account when your offer is accepted. That will assure the seller that you have and can access the cash.

You don't want to put your own lifestyle in jeopardy, but if you do have extra money to invest, consider financing your own flip journey. The more you finance, the less you need to pay back with interest.

Think Creatively

In a way, Wright had something akin to partners when he bought the first home he flipped. He relied on friends to pay rent each month. Their payments covered the mortgage. As noted, though, he was confident he could afford to pay the mortgage, even if friends had to leave the arrangement.

Most people who flip houses don't want to live in that house with others. Still, there are ways to have friends, family, and others invest in your flip. Some people like to invest money but find the low interest rates paid by banks and other institutions disheartening. If you can borrowed money from them, you could potentially offer a higher interest rate than those places.

You can also work out a deal where you each invest a certain amount in the flipping project, divvy up home-flipping duties, and split the net profits.

But once you get to know other real estate professionals, partnerships sometimes make perfect sense.

"I do have a partner now, but I didn't when I was starting out," says McCormick. "He was my first contractor and was doing a lot of my work. After a while, we said, 'Why don't we buy these together?'"

This partnership is ideal because McCormick can handle the financial side and his partner oversees the actual flip.

HINT: One way to gain experience in home flipping is to help fund a successful home flipper, says Wright. If you consider doing that, make sure you choose someone who can show you the success they've had through the years. And, of course, you want an interest rate that is higher than you'd receive from a financial institution but lower than that charged by a hard money lender.

Seek Private Money Lenders

As mentioned earlier, friends, family members, and even colleagues may make excellent investment partners for your home-flipping journey. These are people you know who are looking for investment opportunities that pay higher interest rates than what they currently earn from savings, money market accounts, and other investments. You will need to make the interest rate high enough to entice them, but don't become so generous that you pay out all of your profit. Look at the current interest rates for various investments and then see if you can offer more.

Jot down possible financial partners and the amounts they might lend, along with the expected interest rate, or loan terms in the Possible Private Money Lenders worksheet on the following page (see also page 111).

Possible Private Money Lenders

TOTAL AMOUNT NEEDED:

Possible partner: | Phone/email:

Loan amount: | Interest rate:

Loan terms:

Date contacted/notes:

Possible partner: | Phone/email:

Loan amount: | Interest rate:

Loan terms:

Date contacted/notes:

Possible partner: | Phone/email:

Loan amount: | Interest rate:

Loan terms:

Date contacted/notes:

Consider Your Home Equity

If you own a home, you can likely secure a home equity loan. That is a loan against the value of your property. If you have a home worth $100,000 and you have paid off the mortgage, you should be able to secure a home equity loan for that amount. If you have a home worth $100,000 but have only paid off $50,000 of the mortgage, you should be able to secure a $50,000 loan.

CAVEAT: Remember, a home equity loan will likely cost you money in closing costs and other fees. Plus, if you can't pay the amount of your new loan, the lender may foreclose on your home. And, like any loan, you will pay interest on a home equity loan.

EXPERT ADVICE

Kyle McCormick

"Home equity is the easiest way to extract money for whatever you want," says McCormick. "You are in complete control, and getting it has nothing to do with experience in real estate. Then, if you can get people to lend you money, that's the hardest problem—finance—solved.

Traditional Bank Loans

At the time of this writing, it is difficult to secure bank loans even for primary residences. As the economy and stock market change, so will banks' interest in lending money. Watch the economy and have a discussion with your banker about what you need and why. They may offer a solution that allows you to buy a property and flip it for a decent profit.

There are other ways to finance a flip, including selling a property to another person who flips houses—generally, those are lower risk for the newer investor. Take your time to save money or work with others to secure the financing to begin your journey. List your traditional lending options on the Traditional Lenders worksheet (see also page 112).

Traditional Lenders

Bank name:

Contact name: | Phone/email:

Loan amount: | Interest rate:

Loan terms:

Notes:

Bank name:

Contact name: | Phone/email:

Loan amount: | Interest rate:

Loan terms:

Notes:

Bank name:

Contact name: | Phone/email:

Loan amount: | Interest rate:

Loan terms:

Notes:

Hard Money Lenders

If you're a more experienced home flipper, consider hard money lenders. I don't recommend this option for newbie flippers because the fees are very high. Those that engage hard money lenders quickly flip houses to avoid high interest payments. BiggerPockets.com has an array of information about hard money lenders. Those lenders are most often used by home flippers with solid track records who know they can buy, flip, and resell very quickly. The hard money lenders generally only care about the after-repair value (ARV) of the home. They don't often concern themselves with the seller's financial standing or credit history.

BiggerPockets.com notes that "hard money interest typically ranges between 14 and 20 percent—often with four to six points on top of that—so pay off these loans quickly. While hard money lenders can be a great starting place, there are certainly better funding sources with better rates."

Their example: "If you borrow $100,000 from a hard money lender at 16 percent and it takes six months from start to finish for repayment, your interest charges would be $8,000. Then you must pay 'points.' Four points equals $4,000."

If you hold the flipped property only half that time, your interest charges would be $6K instead of $12K.

CHAPTER 3

Time Is Money

If you buy a home to flip, you know you'll invest a certain amount of money. You will also invest a certain amount of time. And you need to guard that as closely as you do your money. Yes, you can make money by home flipping, but it may take years to do so.

Home flipping is not a quick project. Consider this report by ATTOM Data Solutions:

> *"Homes flips completed in Q4 2018 took an average of 175 days, down from 177 days in the previous quarter and down from 178 days in Q4 2017."*

The report also noted it took even longer in specific markets: Provo, Utah (219 days); Boise, Idaho (215 days); Erie, Pennsylvania (213 days); Gainesville, Florida (213 days); and Kalamazoo, Michigan (212 days).

The Motley Fool broke the process down in this way while noting there are countless variables:

- **ONE TO TWO MONTHS TO BUY THE HOUSE.** You'll spend time searching lists, talking to other investors and/or the realtor you hire (if you hire one), and moving quickly when you find a property that works for you. Although Motley Fool doesn't mention it, you will also spend time checking reviews and lining up contractors.

- **TWO TO THREE MONTHS TO RENOVATE THE HOUSE.** Motley Fool noted if you intend to do most of the work yourself, plan to spend at least four to five days a week there. If you hire contractors, you'll likely spend two to three days a week.

> **TIP:** I like to be on-site most of the time contractors work on my house. I find they sometimes have questions or suggestions. You, of course, can make your own decision.

- **ONE TO TWO MONTHS TO SELL THE HOUSE.** Of course, this varies depending on whether you sell the house yourself or work with a realtor and many other variables.

The Best Ways to Spend Your Time on Home Flipping

No matter your abilities, you likely have or can access several free or affordable time-savers for a successful home flip. My late husband was a superb handyman, as was my dad. That means they could do a lot of work that would otherwise cost hundreds or thousands of dollars to have someone else do.

Home flipper Taylor Jackson of Kentucky and her husband Tommy English have relatives who are contractors and were especially eager to help the millennial couple flip their first investment home. Unlike many first-time home flippers, the couple chose a historic home to flip and resell. But they did plenty of planning first. "The house we chose is structurally sound," she says. "We looked at some smaller houses that would have been easier to remodel but had a ton of structural issues, which was going to be much more complicated to renovate. Before we bought the house, we put together a budget. So we actually knew what that renovation budget was going to be before we made an offer on the house. That changed a little bit over time, but not much. We concentrated on what we absolutely had to spend. So we have to put in electricity. We have to put in heat. We have to put in plumbing. Then we could say, 'What are the things that we would like to spend on?'"

Even then, the couple was careful not to overspend on fixtures and other items for the home. They bought some higher-ticket items on Black Friday and at similar sales. And they stuck to the plan of what they would replace and what they would not touch.

Consider these ideas of the most profitable ways to spend your time when you flip a home.

- DEMOLITION. This might sound easy, but there are areas you should not do yourself, such as removing asbestos. You should also avoid walls or other areas that might impact the home's structure or any utilities. If you can do what is called "light demolition," that will save you money. That includes removing carpeting, cabinets, and even floorboards. When Jackson and English bought their home, the heavy demolition was already complete. They were also able to check with contractors in their family to determine what areas you can take on yourself without harming the home's integrity.

- RENOVATION. Check for free in-person or online classes at your local home goods store. You can often learn how to do plaster work, strip woodwork, and fix tile.

- PAINT. Painting a home isn't easy and can be physically taxing. If you are fit enough, though, painting the interior of your own home can save you thousands of dollars. Remember, too, that you can paint part of the home—such as the walls—and hire someone to do the trim, ceilings, and other more labor-intensive spots.

- BUY YOUR OWN APPLIANCES AND OTHER MATERIALS. This isn't always a smart move. Sometimes contractors can get you better bargains than you can find on your own, thanks to professional discounts and insider knowledge. Jackson and her husband bought their own appliances by shopping sales during key times. She estimated that saved them hundreds of dollars.

> **TIP:** Check with a contractor before buying materials such as tiles. They will often point you to a relatively unknown but quality supplier and/or help you determine the amount of material that is needed.

- DO AS MUCH OF YOUR OWN LANDSCAPING AS POSSIBLE. You can transform a home's curb appeal with trimmed bushes and trees, cut grass, and strategic placement of mulch and potted flowers. Research what plants grow best in your area. You can usually find out just by talking to neighbors and looking at their yards. Then plan how to pull the yard together and begin.

Of course, you also want to spend your time in areas that don't involve hands-on renovation. Some of those areas include:

- **SEARCHING FOR PROPERTY AND/OR DEALS.** The last house I found was actually a for-sale-by-owner home that popped up on a minor website. My realtor wouldn't have known about it because it wasn't on the MLS. So don't rely entirely on someone else to find you a property. Spend your time searching too. Track what you find and jot down the address, list price, estimated cost of renovations, expected net income, and realtor information on a form like this:

Homes to Consider

Address:

List price:	Estimated renovation cost:	Expected net income:
Realtor/owner:	Contact information:	

Notes:

See page 114 for a Homes to Consider worksheet you can use.

2. NEGOTIATING. There are some things you probably won't be able to negotiate, such as the cost of appliances. When a big box store sells a product, they will rarely negotiate (though you may have some luck on less-than-perfect items). Of course, you'll negotiate for the price of the home you purchase. You should also spend your time negotiating contractor fees, landscaping fees, and even realtor fees. You won't know what's possible if you don't ask.

3. EDUCATE YOURSELF ABOUT MARKETING. Sure, when your house is ready to sell, you can use traditional methods such as word of mouth and signs. If you sell with an agent, they will also market your home. It's a good idea to learn some basic online marketing skills too. One of the most effective involves SEO, or search engine optimization. Much of that consists of understanding what terms to use to draw online buyers to your listings. There are many free courses and resources available to help you learn enough basics to successfully boost your listing's online viewing.

4. WATCH YOUR BUDGET. We've all had moments when we didn't pay strict attention to our expenses. You do not want to slip in this manner when you flip a house. Buy a basic budgeting program, make one yourself on Excel, or use basic budget trackers like the examples starting on page 16. See page 92 for budget trackers you can fill out or copy as many times as you need. Then log all of your expenses carefully so you know how much you've spent and how much you have. Sometimes, though, you won't have time to immediately log your expenses. Use the following worksheet to jot down expenses until you can log them in your official spreadsheet or tally.

Use a Daily Expense Form like the following to track expenses until you have time to tally them on a formal spreadsheet. See also page 113 for a copy of this form.

Daily Expense Form

Date:	Purchase:	Cost:	Category:

Notes:

Date:	Purchase:	Cost:	Category:

Notes:

Date:	Purchase:	Cost:	Category:

Notes:

Date:	Purchase:	Cost:	Category:

Notes:

Date:	Purchase:	Cost:	Category:

Notes:

Date:	Purchase:	Cost:	Category:

Notes:

5. SHOP FOR EXPERTS. Realtors usually recommend a home inspector and title company. They will likely also talk to you about homeowners' insurance. Rather than blindly follow the agent's advice, it's smart to read about your area's local requirements and shop for a good deal, just as you would for contractors. Keep track of home inspector recommendations you gather on a sheet like this (see page 115 for a Possible Home Inspectors worksheet you can use):

Possible Home Inspectors

Name:	Phone/email:
Company name:	Address:
Fee:	Availability:
Notes:	

Name:	Phone/email:
Company name:	Address:
Fee:	Availability:
Notes:	

CHAPTER 4

Your Foundation/ Legwork

As you plan to buy a house to flip, it's imperative to remember you are (usually) not looking for a house to live in. You are looking for a house to renovate and sell for a net profit. And the most important point—you need to follow the budget you set.

Every dollar you go above the budget is a dollar you're taking from your profit, and initially, from your bank account. I've said before, house flipping is nowhere near as quick and easy as it seems on some reality shows. It will take money and may take years to sell the house. Can you pay the mortgage, taxes, and upkeep during that time? Yes, if you stick to your budget.

So how do you decide where to buy the first house you'll flip? If you're like my parents or my late husband and me, you'll choose the area you already live in. We knew that we were investing in neighborhoods where real estate values were either steady or rising, and where homes with good bones just needed some tender, loving care. Sure, other areas may offer greater potential than where you live, but convenience is key when you begin your home-flipping journey.

TIP: When selecting the area in which you'll buy, don't avoid those that frequently have houses for sale. The last house I sold—and earned a 30 percent net profit on—was in a neighborhood where two other houses were for sale. Each sold almost immediately. The reason? The houses were located in a highly desirable area, particularly for Federal government employees who often bought there but moved when administrations changed. Talk to people in the area you select and ask if there are times when more houses turn over.

Of course, that doesn't mean you should assume that an area with a steady stream of houses for sale is desirable. Do your homework and research the following:

- Look at houses that are currently under contract in the area you select. Remember you are competing against other sellers. You may need to lower your asking price.

- Research how many houses sold in that neighborhood in recent months, how long they were on the market, and how the sales rate compared with the asking prices. You especially want to find those that sold right away at the price you hope to set for your flipped home.

- Look at homes that have been on the market for long periods of time. If a home has lingered on the market, this could mean it's overpriced, the area is undesirable, there are structural problems in the home, or another negative aspect. Again, these houses should be in your targeted area and sale price.

Use the following Competition Log to track those homes (see also page 118 for another copy of the Competition Log).

Competition Log

HOMES THAT SOLD QUICKLY

Address:

| List price: | Sales price: | Days on the market: |

Notes:

HOMES THAT ARE STUCK ON THE MARKET

Address:

| List price: | Sales price: | Days on the market: |

Notes:

HOMES UNDER CONTRACT

Address:

| List price: | Sales price: | Days on the market: |

Notes:

How to Pinpoint an Area

Of course, you can work with a realtor. They have access to the MLS, so they can often find homes much faster than you could on your own. And they know the ins and outs of contracts, homeowners' association requirements, insurance choices, and much more. Before you work with a realtor, though, it helps to narrow down the area and perhaps the neighborhood where you want to buy.

The Areas for Consideration worksheet (on the next page and page 121) helps you prepare a basic list of considerations to compare the areas you've selected. You can find statistics and demographic information through resources like school district websites, parent boards, city websites, etc.

Finding out the property's livability score can be very helpful in making your decision. A livability score is based on an analysis of seven categories: housing, neighborhood, transportation, environment, health, engagement, and opportunity. Scores range from zero to one hundred. You can find livability scores at Livability.com.

Areas for Consideration

Area name:

Median income:	Median age:	Crime rate:

Livability score: | School ratings:

Notes:

Area name:

Median income:	Median age:	Crime rate:

Livability score: | School ratings:

Notes:

Area name:

Median income:	Median age:	Crime rate:

Livability score: | School ratings:

Notes:

Area name:

Median income:	Median age:	Crime rate:

Livability score: | School ratings:

Notes:

Some points you want to check as you look at areas:

- How does the neighborhood look? Are lawns overgrown? Are homes in disrepair? Are junk cars parked on the roads?

- What do current owners say? Do they like it there? Would they buy there again?

- What do business owners say? Is business solid? Are they frustrated by crime, taxes, or a nonresponsive local government?

Hunting for Your House

There are many ways to find the house you want to flip. But remember the old saying: "You make your money when you buy, not when you sell." That means you need to get the best deal possible to earn any profit. If the deal isn't right, there's no sense buying.

So how do you begin? Contact a realtor for the most up-to-date listings on the MLS. You can also research "for sale by owner" properties or visit online auctions. Another option is to wholesale your flipped house to other flippers. Let's look more in depth at these possibilities.

YOUR REALTOR. Again, a realtor can help quickly target homes that you might like, simply by using the MLS.

"The realtor's MLS access means you can instantly know when a property is listed," says Lucas Machado of House Heroes. "If you are on your own looking on Zillow or Redfin—there is a delay. You might only see it on Zillow or Redfin two days after it's listed."

That means you can lose out. A realtor can also take care of contracts, negotiations, and other details that most first-time real estate investors aren't savvy enough to handle well.

Use this form to keep track of realtor leads (see page 122 for a copy of this form). In addition to the home-buying process, realtors can help match you with other service providers. Feel free to use the notes column to record memorable points about the realtors you connect with.

Realtor Information

Realtor's name	Company	Phone	Email	Additional notes

FOR SALE BY OWNER. I bought my current house from an owner. I found the home, but I let my realtor handle the negotiations and sale. Why didn't I negotiate on my own? Even though I have bought and sold several homes, there are many contracts, insurance policies, and regulations that need to be executed appropriately. My agent did all of that for me, plus I could insist on specific fixes and changes.

> **TIP:** You can find homes that owners are selling on ForSalebyOwner.com, Zillow.com, and other websites.

ONLINE AUCTIONS. You'll find many websites dedicated to selling homes via auction. Those homes may be in foreclosure or part of an estate. Some of the best-known are Auction.com, Hubzu.com, and Treasury.gov/auctions/treasury/rp/.

Many homes that are auctioned are either in foreclosure by the bank or lender, or were seized by a government entity for unpaid taxes. Auctions are a risky way to buy a home, especially if you're a newcomer to investment. Consider these tips before you begin your auction search:

- Understand the required fees and obligations you undertake when you use such a site.

- Most auction companies do not allow prospective buyers to have any type of home inspection before buying.

- Do not bid on or buy such a home if you can't find out if there are liens against it, as any profits from the sale go to satisfying those creditors first.

WHOLESALING TO OTHER FLIPPERS. Real estate investors looking to wholesale properties must find properties worth flipping and get them under contract. They negotiate the terms with the seller, such as closing costs and purchase price. Next, they find a house-flipping investor to purchase the property and complete the rehab.

Wholesalers make money several ways. One involves a negotiated "spread," which is the difference between the buy price and the sell price. They can also make money based on a fixed percentage of the final sale—i.e., when the flipper sells to the end buyer. This could range from 5 to 10 percent. As a wholesaler, you don't take ownership of the property or do any rehab yourself, making wholesaling an easy way to start flipping homes without any money.

Wholesale successfully by building up a group of investors or contacts interested in flipping houses. Then, your job is done after negotiating a deal with the seller. The investor handles the closing and rehab.

EXPERT ADVICE

Erik Wright

Erik Wright of Tennessee takes sound advice from other investors and property managers.

"I really find out the best areas by talking to property managers. I can't personally know everything about all the different areas in a city. I would rather just go to somebody smarter than me who learns about the area for a living," he says. "I want to know what they say. I get their advice, and I go from there."

TIP: Learn as much as you can about the market and real estate. An abundance of education is available for free, even at seminars. "At some of those classes, there are people trying to sell you stuff. Just go with the mindset of 'I'm not here to buy anything. I'm here to learn and just kind of see what other people are doing,'" says Castro-Socas.

CHAPTER 5

Assembling Your Team

One of the costliest mistakes some home flippers, including my parents, make is to believe they need little or no help doing the work to renovate a property. Many think DIY is a great strategy to save money when, in fact, it may cost them more. Successful home flippers are often the people who have built a reliable team of contractors, realtors, financial experts, plumbers, electricians, and other real estate experts. Or they have a dedicated team that knows how to find the specialists they need in a hurry.

Experienced tradespeople can keep you from paying steep prices when buying a property, deciding what renovations are needed, choosing materials, staging the home for sale, and much more.

My dad had acquired many carpentry and handyman skills throughout the years. He put plenty of sweat equity in the property he bought to flip. He installed windows, added insulation, braced floors, and cleared a well. The downside was that he often tackled time-consuming jobs. He was still working at a full-time, stressful job at the time, and the work took a toll on his health.

If he'd hired tradespeople, he would have saved himself many headaches, months of work, and likely, money. Skilled, experienced tradespeople can do the job in much less time than even the savviest amateurs.

"Some of the biggest failures are, to some extent, cutting corners," says Machado. "Much of what we do is very complicated. You have to have a good team around you to succeed. People try to save money and increase profitability by worrying about things that aren't important. They go with the cheaper guy or don't want to pay for an estimate....Don't be afraid to make less money and have more resources at your disposal. You make your money when you buy, when you find a real estate deal you bought at a great price, not because you saved 10 percent on a renovation."

That's not to say you shouldn't do any work on your own. If you have the time and skills to hang lighting fixtures, refinish cabinets, paint walls, or any other task, by all means, do it. But don't take on more than you can realistically handle.

Remember, too, that contractors, landscapers, and other professionals can usually obtain discounts that you can't—usually at 15 to 20 percent off retail on items you need. Here are some other things to consider about that point:

TIP: You might not see a huge discount on products bought by tradespeople, but you do save. When a contractor sends someone to buy and transport the products to your project, that costs them money. They need to pay for gas, the products, and the worker's time. Sure, you can buy your own renovation materials, but you likely won't save any money. Plus, you'll spend your valuable time doing it.

REMINDER: Contractors know what you need. Have you ever shopped for an item you need, only to get it home and realize that you bought the wrong size or model? Have you ever wondered what the highest quality product is and if it's worth your money? When a contractor, under your direction, buys a product for you, they know what you need. And they understand quality. Plus, they can better estimate how many tiles, carpet squares, tubing materials, or whatever else you need. Take advantage of their expertise, and let them shop for you.

ANOTHER BONUS: Contractors will usually handle the process of securing permits, HOA approvals, and other time-consuming administrative work.

How Do You Find Great Contractors?

If you already own a home, you have likely worked with contractors throughout the years. When I bought my current home in Austin, Texas, I didn't know any contractors in the state. My realtor suggested a few. The painter she recommended dripped paint, missed areas, and otherwise did a shoddy job. Plus, he overcharged me.

The general contractor my realtor recommended to install a shower in the master bath was the opposite. He listened to what I wanted, made suggestions that saved me money, and even met me at a tile store to help me choose floor tile patterns that complemented the wall tile but met my budget constraints. Yes, I have hired him again. And he's referred me to other top-notch contractors. On the other hand, I avoid those that receive bad references.

How do you find a contractor that does high-quality work?

1. ASK YOUR TRUSTED CONTRACTOR. As with any other profession, contractors know each other by reputation, if not name. They are usually happy to refer their clients to other contractors who they know do high-quality work.

2. LOOK AT REVIEWS. Do a search and you'll find online profiles for many contractors. Once you've narrowed the list down to a select group of potential hires, ask them for other references. One contractor invited me to come to a client's home, talk to the client, and inspect the work.

3. ASK THE REFERENCES POINTED QUESTIONS. Is the contractor on time? Does he return calls and texts? Does he have the right tools?

4. TALK TO OTHER INVESTORS. There are plenty of investors in your area, and most are likely more than willing to share contractor names with you. When they get their best contractors more work, they win points with those contractors.

The contractor you hire should have the time, expertise, and tools to handle the jobs you need completed. When you contact a contractor, take notes about your conversation. Use the Assessing Contractors worksheet to easily find information on each contractor you contact (see page 123 for a copy of this worksheet).

Assessing Contractors

Name: | Company name:

Specialty:

Contact information:

Was the contractor on time? | Does the contractor return calls and messages?

Does the contractor have the right tools and knowledge?

Was the estimate accurate? | Did the contractor conduct follow-up checks?

Notes:

Name: | Company name:

Specialty:

Contact information:

Was the contractor on time? | Does the contractor return calls and messages?

Does the contractor have the right tools and knowledge?

Was the estimate accurate? | Did the contractor conduct follow-up checks?

Notes:

"You honestly don't know right away if you have a good contractor. It's really a case of trial and error," says McCormick, who had to fire a contractor at one point. "My best bit of advice would be to understand their scope, make sure they understand their scope, and put them on a timeline. If they don't adhere to 'get those done by the end of this week,' 'get this done by the end of that week,' fire them and move on."

Types of Contractors

You know electricians are different from plumbers, but there are other categories of contractors and tradespeople you'll want to know about before you hire them to renovate your home.

Licensed Contractors

Not every contractor is licensed. It's important to know who is and isn't. Most licensed contractors have liability insurance that protects you and your family from personal injury and property damage. I am especially cautious when hiring electricians and plumbers. Do not be shy about asking what insurance they carry.

Handypeople

Some licensed contractors grow weary of working for companies and strike out on their own as handypeople. They often can do many tasks, such as hanging lights, installing faucets, and repairing drywall. Remember, though, the person is no longer a contractor so may not have licenses or insurance that cover their work when they install electrical wires, repair water systems, or repair air conditioners.

Tips for Hiring a Contractor

A company that uses project managers may be a bit more expensive, but you generally receive extra service too. The project manager will monitor the work done, notify you of any problems, and work with you to resolve them. The project manager can also send a different contractor to your site if support is needed.

There's nothing wrong with directly hiring a contractor. My late husband and I used an electrician who had worked in the area for years. In fact, he was an apprentice electrician when our home was built. That meant he knew a lot of the ins and outs of the wiring. He was timely and honest, and charged a fair price. If you decide to hire a contractor, keep these points in mind:

- **PUT EVERYTHING IN WRITING.** Even if you have a history with the contractor or the company, make sure you have everything in writing. This will protect you and will be useful when you resell the property. A written contract shows what was done and how the work was completed. It may also be useful for tax purposes.

- **CONFIRM THAT THE CONTRACTOR WILL BE RESPONSIBLE FOR PERMITS AND PAPERWORK.** Make sure the contractor is responsible for permits and other paperwork needed to complete your job. That will save you time and headaches.

- **PUT THE CLEANUP RESPONSIBILITY IN THE CONTRACT.** Cleanup is important and part of a contractor's job. I've played the trusting person several times and believed that cleanup would be done. It wasn't. And because it wasn't in the contract, I was stuck scrubbing and finding someone to haul junk away. Learn from my mistakes and put cleanup responsibilities in writing.

- **CHECK LICENSES AND INSURANCE COVERAGE.** Yes, this goes for those that you've hired in the past. Things change in people's work, and they may honestly forget to tell you that they are no longer licensed to do something. As you plan, check to make sure the person you hire is licensed and insured for the job they're doing.

- **SPELL OUT PAYMENT.** Do you pay by credit card? Check? Do you pay a deposit and then make payments at set intervals? Who receives payment? Are you responsible for all supplies, or will the contractor provide them? What if you're not happy with the work? When is final payment due? Make sure you know exactly how and when payment is expected and your recourse for less-than-stellar work. And definitely, put it in writing.

Your Realtor Is Vital

It's smart to use the same type of due diligence to hire a realtor that you would use to hire a contractor. (Please refer to the Realtor Information worksheet on page 42 to keep track of realtor leads.)

A realtor doesn't become successful unless they have the expertise to steer clients to top properties at prices that fit their budgets. Standard practice calls for the seller of a property to pay the cost of realtors. Even if you need to pay a modest fee, it is often wise for to work with realtors when looking for properties to flip. There are many other things realtors can help you with. Those include:

- Finding homes you don't know about. Realtors continually drive around various areas, prospecting for homes. They also attend meetings with other realtors to talk about locations, properties, and other relevant topics.

- Understanding the pros and cons of specific areas, such as flood zones, high-crime areas, and areas in decline.

- They have the inside track on offers and counteroffers. Their network of colleagues provides them with insights on what the market will bear.

How to Choose a Realtor

Consider some of these ideas before you sign with an agent.

- Ask your friends and family for references. Networking is one of the best ways to find a quality realtor.

- Do research about the realtor. Read online reviews and ask for references from the realtor's past customers.

- Talk to several realtors. Find the one you most enjoy working with and then ask about their fees. Don't hesitate to negotiate.

- Read the contract. Don't think that just because you get along with someone, you won't have conflicts. Find out exactly how you can cancel a contract and what penalties might be involved.

CHAPTER 6

The Property Search

As noted earlier, realtors can guide you toward the best areas to flip a house. If you want the agent's commitment to your project, consider allowing them to handle both sides of the sale. If they find you a home to purchase and then represent your home sale, that will give them more incentives to work hard for you. Of course your realtor will have other clients, so try to work out a reasonable schedule.

EXPERT ADVICE

Lucas Machado

"It varies for everyone," says Lucas Machado of the best way to search for a house. "When a property sells on the MLS, it will sell for the most the market pays for the home. There isn't a lot of room for negotiation. For me, I like buying a home directly from homeowners. There's less competition, and we can also be more picky because we get so many opportunities, and we don't have time to look at everything."

Consider these ideas to see a high number of properties without burdening your agent:

- **ATTEND OPEN HOUSES.** If you're interested in looking at a number of houses to explore points you like and don't like, consider going to open houses without your realtor. You can look at homes, take notes and photos, and discuss them with your realtor without making the realtor spend time on a property you wouldn't consider.

- **DRIVE AROUND THE NEIGHBORHOOD.** Look beyond a potential house to the neighborhood in which its located. You want to see how people care for their lawns, if homes are maintained, and if you see any major downsides to the vicinity. View the neighborhood as a potential resident. For example, you likely would not want to buy on a busy street, and it might be undesirable for potential buyers. Other turnoffs include areas filled with homes that are rentals or that have views blocked by utility wires.

- **KEEP AN EYE OUT FOR HOMES THAT MIGHT BE VACANT.** Signs might include a poorly maintained yard, trash cans sitting outside, and packages by the front door. Talk with neighbors and you may discover a home that will soon go up for sale. Sometimes buyers have had a family problem, a job transfer, or another issue that makes them want to sell fast. That could be a chance to snag a high-quality property before it goes on the market.

When determining a property's potential for flipping, remember these tips:

- **LOOK FOR HOMES THAT ARE UGLY ON THE INSIDE.** Just because a home has dated appliances, rooms that are painted with weird colors, or stained carpets doesn't mean it won't be a great home to flip. In fact, it might be one of the best properties for you. If a home has great bones but needs some TLC, it can be a home flippers dream.

- **LOOK FOR HOMES THAT ARE UGLY ON THE OUTSIDE.** The same goes for homes with no curb appeal. Just because an owner doesn't take care of the yard, hasn't replaced windows, or hasn't replaced the front door doesn't mean the house lacks potential. Again, these homes can be a home flipper's dream, and those minor flaws can often hide hidden jewels.

- **LOCATION, LOCATION, LOCATION.** As I've mentioned, potential buyers look for specific amenities. If you're flipping a one-bedroom condo, access to major employers, public transportation, and a post office are likely key amenities for potential buyers. Those same buyers might find closeness to a school or playground a negative. Of course, if you're renovating a five-bedroom detached home, close proximity to schools, playgrounds, parks, and stores are almost certainly selling points.

Use the Possible Properties worksheet to determine places you might want to see. (See page 125 for another copy of this worksheet.)

Possible Properties

Address:

Asking price:	Realtor/owner:	Contact information:

Notes:

Address:

Asking price:	Realtor/owner:	Contact information:

Notes:

Address:

Asking price:	Realtor/owner:	Contact information:

Notes:

Address:

Asking price:	Realtor/owner:	Contact information:

Notes:

Address:

Asking price:	Realtor/owner:	Contact information:

Notes:

Is This the One to Renovate?

Absolutely do not make an offer on a home until you decide it fits your renovation budget and plans. Are you concerned you'll lose the home in a hot market? That could certainly happen, which is why you want to begin to inspect and estimate renovation costs as early as the first time you visit. No matter how attractive the home, if it doesn't fit your budget or plans, it is not the one for you.

Fortunately, if you plan how to examine homes for investment property potential, you can quickly determine if the home may be right for you. This section covers some fairly obvious red flags you'll want to avoid as well as features that might indicate you've found a diamond in the rough.

> **TIP:** It's always a great idea to bring someone with you when you tour a home. Sure, you can likely get a feel for it when you go alone. But, oftentimes, one person might see something another does not. That's especially true if you have a realtor, home inspector, contractor, or a real-estate savvy friend.

> **TIP:** Your top concern when inspecting an investment property is making sure it is structurally sound. Second, try to determine if the renovations needed fit your budget. You may be able to stretch your budget if more work is needed than you're prepared to do. You can require the seller to do the work as a condition of the sale. Don't bank on that, though.

There are different ways you can inspect the house during your initial tour. Remember, this does not take the place of a professional inspection before you buy. This research is just the first step in determining if the property might work for you.

What you need:

- A cell camera

- A voice recorder and/or pen and paper

- A flashlight to look into closets and under sinks

If you're like me, you take photos of prospective homes and then have a heck of a time figuring out what you meant to show. When you go to look at a home, record or write down notes with each photo you take. Then compile the voice recordings and photos for each house in a separate folder. It's easy to become so caught up in the excitement of looking at a home—especially if other potential buyers are there—that you neglect to do this. If you can remember to follow this method, though, it'll save you time in the long run.

After you tour the home, you can look back through your photos and notes as you determine what fixes are needed or discuss the home with your realtor, contractor, home inspector, or the potential seller. They will assess your findings and offer advice.

When you are looking to flip your first, second, or even third house, you likely want to find a property that is fairly easy to renovate and resell. Remember, it's not your goal to make the house fit into your budget and plans. It's your goal to find a home that already does. And that means avoiding a home that needs or may have the potential for costly fixes that are out of your budget.

Red Flags

Walk away if you come across any of the following issues:

- **IFFY STRUCTURAL ISSUES.** Even though you'll have access to a home inspection before you buy, it will save you time and heartache to check the home's foundation, floors, and walls. Look for cracks, uneven or "spongy" floors, rotten wood, cracked tile, and door frames that seem out of position. These may all be signs of structural deficiencies.

- **TERMITES, PESTS, AND VERMIN.** When you tour a home, keep an ear out for scratching sounds and watch for pellet droppings. Those could be signs of mice, rats, and other rodents. Droppings could also be signs of cockroaches. Pay close attention to wood on fences and decks. If you tap on them or on wooden walls, listen to the sound. If it's hollow, it could indicate termites. Another idea: shine the light from your mobile phone into dark areas such as closets. Pests and rodents tend to gather and disperse when light appears.

- **MOLD.** Look under kitchen and bathroom sinks, in corners, and near the hot water heater and sump pump. Do you smell the musty odor of mold? Take note. Many times you can see fuzzy, slimy spots of green, black, white, and other colors. Mold is difficult to remove and can cause major health problems. NOTE: Leaking pipes and windows can also lead to mold.

- **PLUMBING ISSUES.** If you see water spots on the ceiling, hear gurgling pipes, or notice slow-running drains, the home could have faulty plumbing. That is more than a nuisance; it can signal major—and costly—problems, such as a sewer line backup.

- **SMALL KITCHEN.** An outdated kitchen is one thing. Appliances, sinks, and tiles can be replaced. A small kitchen can't be changed just like that. And if it is enlarged, this usually costs major money. Again, if you're flipping a one-bedroom condominium, a small kitchen may not be an issue. If you're flipping a home for more than one person, it may well be a deal breaker for potential buyers.

- **ONE FULL BATHROOM.** This one has a caveat: a 500-square-foot condo (yes, they're out there) likely won't have more than a full bathroom. For a family, though, you'll likely have a tough time selling a home with just one full bath, as you'll see in many mid-century homes. Modern buyers generally want more.

- **WATER SPOTS ON THE CEILINGS.** Again, water spots may indicate a roof needs to be replaced. That's an expensive fix you want to avoid.

- **THE TOILET MOVES.** That can indicate water damage and a rotting floor.

- **AN OBSTRUCTED VIEW.** I once looked at a home in Arizona that was perfect except for aboveground wires that were visible from the living room. I passed. The wires didn't bother me at all, but I knew that when I resold the house, potential buyers might balk. A backyard is also important. I considered flipping a third-floor condo with a large balcony. The problem? The balcony had a direct view of a neighbor's many garbage cans. Pass.

Warning Signs

The following warning signs indicate that Houston, we may have a problem. While all warning signs should be considered, they aren't as critical as red flags, which are usually deal breakers.

- **BROKEN WINDOWS OR DOORS.** Look for cracks, chips, and warped wood around windows and doors. Make sure the doors and windows open easily. Any of these problems may lead to expensive fixes. You'll want to check with a home inspector or contractor to be sure, but be prepared to walk away.

- **VERY LITTLE HOT WATER.** This could be as simple as the temperature gauge on the hot water being turned low. It could also mean the hot water heater is not properly installed or needs replacement.

- **LIGHT SWITCHES THAT DON'T WORK.** A breaker could have tripped, shutting off power. That's easy to fix. However, a nonworking outlet could also signal serious electrical problems in the home.

Promising Highlights

- **CROWN MOLDING.** Crown molding adds a touch of class to the home. If it's chipped or dim, a fresh coat of paint can usually brighten it right up.

- **A LARGE KITCHEN.** You can easily renovate many things in a house, but a small a kitchen is not among them. If you find a home with a large, airy kitchen, you're in luck.

- **LARGE, MODERN BATHROOMS.** Sure, you can renovate a bathroom, but it's costly, even if you do a lot of work yourself. I've done at least eight. Three were full remodels, two were half remodels. All of that work was done by contractors. The other three bathrooms were half remodels done jointly by me and a contractor. None were completed for under $6,000. Of course, that price will change depending on many variables. Suffice it to say that if you find a home with large, modern bathrooms, you're in luck again!

- **WORN CARPET.** That's generally an easy and cost-effective fix.

- **UGLY LIGHT FIXTURES.** It's relatively easy to swap light fixtures. Many stylish fixtures are available at bargain prices.

Other Considerations

- **PROPERTY TAXES.** These will vary greatly depending on the home's specific locale. Research them carefully so you can budget for them. The current owner or the area's tax assessment office should supply you with the information. If the home is managed under an HOA, you may also get the information from their property manager.

- **PLANNED DEVELOPMENT.** It's always a good idea to check out the planned development in the area of interest. Will there be new housing that can compete with your property when you sell? Are residential areas now slated for commercial zoning? These variables may impact the future sale price of the home.

- **IS THERE HIGH OWNER TURNOVER?** People can be mobile, but a consistent number of "For Sale" signs in front of homes is often an indication there is a problem in the area (see page 54). Talk to owners of other homes and local investors to determine if there's a characteristic in the vicinity that makes it less than desirable.

- **IS THE HOME IN A FLOOD ZONE?** Is it in the path of hurricanes? Is there a high likelihood for earthquakes in the region? Understand where you're buying. Even if the area were to avoid a natural disaster, you would likely pay high insurance costs.

- **IS THE ASSESSMENT LOW?** Even if you plan to pay with cash, you want to have the property assessed before you buy. A low appraisal warns banks that they may not want to lend a certain amount for the purchase price. The same low assessment should also be a red flag for you. If the sales price and assessment figures differ by a few hundred or thousand dollars, that's usually not a warning. If the number is further off, you likely want to walk away.

- **ARE THERE LIENS OR OWNER DISPUTES?** Before you buy a property, you or your realtor will do a title search of the property. That will tell you who owns it and if there are financial liens on the property. If ownership is questionable, you could become ensnared in a legal battle. Any liens against the property must be paid for the owner to sell the property. Such dicey situations indicate you should move on.

- **WAS THE HOME BURGLARIZED IN THE PAST?** Was it a crime site? Research that information before you buy. Future potential buyers might shy away from such properties.

- **HOW LONG HAS THE HOME BEEN ON THE MARKET?** Has it turned over frequently? Ask these questions before you commit. There could be a problem with the home that you have not yet found.

The Home Inspection

You absolutely want to order a home inspection before you buy a home. The buyer pays for the inspection unless an agreement with the seller is made ahead of time. We'll discuss that more in a later chapter. You will sometimes go up against potential buyers who make an offer with a "no inspection" clause. Do not do that. You can and likely will learn a lot during your inspection of the home, especially if a real estate professional joins you. But the best walk-through in the world may not find many serious problems. Those can include an improperly installed hot water heater, an HVAC system that needs replacement, a roof that is near the end of its life, and many other issues that can spell major costs.

Use the Home Inspection Information worksheet to write down things you want the inspector to be sure to check. Take notes on it on the day of the inspection. (See also page 115 for a copy of the Possible Home Inspectors worksheet and page 126 for a copy of the Home Inspection Information worksheet.)

Home Inspection Information

Inspector name: | Contact information:

EXTERIOR

Roof: | Gutters:

Other areas:

INTERIOR

Appliances: | HVAC: | Hot water heater:

Other areas:

OTHER QUESTIONS/NOTES

CHAPTER 7

The Work Begins

You've devised your budget, found your team, made a schedule, decided what work you and your team will do, determined your financing source to pay for the property and project, and found and bought the property.

Now it's *go* time.

The sooner you begin the renovation, the sooner you can put the house on the market and recoup your costs—plus, hopefully, a profit.

The problem is that it's easy to become distracted. Doubt it? Think about a time when you stopped into a supermarket to buy a carton of milk. Did you just go in, get the milk, pay, and leave? Probably not. You may have stopped by the bakery to see what new desserts were available, checked the sale aisle, and maybe even bought a greeting card. You may have even left and forgotten to buy the milk!

That's why many of us consider a grocery list a true essential. When you tackle a major investment project, such as flipping a home for profit, it's even easier to become sidetracked. A list of priorities is essential.

The Statement of Work (SOW)

You'll hear people talk about SOW (statement of work) documents. The SOW is a step-by-step, detailed document showing the steps you take, from taking the keys to the house to handing the keys to the buyer of the home after you've renovated it. Just because the SOW has a specific name doesn't mean it needs to be in a specific format.

You can make it as long or as short as you want. And if you plan a mainly cosmetic makeover, your SOW can be basic. Just remember, it is your road map to complete the renovations you need on schedule and on budget.

If you've followed the worksheets and suggestions in the book until now, you already have a good idea of what renovations your investment property needs. The reason I say "a good idea" is because you may have found some unexpected challenges you need to address, like a broken garbage disposal, clogged drain, or cracked window.

Build time into your schedule in case of delays. You may want to spend the time between when your offer is accepted and the closing date to write your SOW.

So what is most important to include in your SOW? That depends on your potential buyer. Do you think the buyer will be a first-time homeowner? A young family? An affluent couple? Seniors? This is where your realtor or other investors come in. They will know the best potential buyers for your home and what they will likely value.

How do you write one? Again, there's no one right way, but check out the worksheet to follow to begin to develop your own SOW. (See page 127 for a copy of this sample SOW worksheet.)

Statement of Work (SOW)

Company name:	Contractor name:
Contractor's phone number:	Contractor's email address:

Company mailing address:

Project:

Description:		Due date:	
Products needed	Brand	Cost	Delivery date
1			
2			
3			
4			
		Total cost:	

Project:

Description:		Due date:	
Products needed	Brand	Cost	Delivery date
1			
2			
3			
4			
		Total cost:	

Additional contractor fees:

Expenses:			
1			
2			
3			
Mileage/travel:			
1			
2			
3			
Contract modifications:			
Project	Modification		
1			
2			
3			
Termination date:			

In addition to using a SOW, I've found the following steps helpful:

- **USE A CALENDAR.** I prefer a paper calendar. When I initially speak to the contractors, I work with them to estimate how long each part of the jobs will take. I also plot out how long I need to do my parts of the renovation. Of course I add in some extra days for the work. Delays happen. I also schedule days for cleanup. Then I count out when I can feasibly plan to put the house on the market. That helps the realtor plan too.

- **MAP OUT PRIORITIES.** Tackle the major items first. For example, if you plan to replace a tub with a shower and then do strictly cosmetic renovations after that, plan the bathroom work first. Then you can replace lighting fixtures, change electrical outlet plates, and mow the lawn.

> **TIP:** Most contractors prefer to work alone, without other contractors on-site. If you plan to have two contractors on-site at one time, it is courteous to alert them. Also remember, some contractors need to do things such as turn off the electricity or water. Make sure any contractors that overlap won't be stalled by such protocols.

- **MAKE TWO MASTER LISTS.** The first one is of all the renovations you have planned. Include the supplies you or your contractor will buy for each project. Add the name of the contractor you will use for each task. Leave space for notes. A sample Planned Renovations worksheet for the kitchen is on page 69. See page 129 for blank Planned Renovations worksheets you can fill in for all areas of the house.

  Now create a second master list of contractors that includes the information shown in the example on page 70. See page 142 for a Contractor List worksheet you can fill in.

- **WRITE THINGS DOWN FOR YOUR CONTRACTOR.** It's easy for contractors and landscapers to lose track of the details of your project. Hopefully they are organized. If they're not, though, it can stall your whole project. Don't take a chance. Keep your own list.

- **DON'T LEAVE ANYTHING TO CHANCE.** It's easy to assume that because you have explained everything and written it down, everyone understands the plan. Don't take anything for granted. Check and double-check all of the work. Doing so will help you *and* your contractor. There's nothing worse than waving good-bye to a contractor only to find work was done incorrectly. In fairness, you may not have explained a particular detail.

- **REMEMBER, IT'S YOUR DECISION.** Contractors, landscapers, and other professionals will offer you many suggestions. In fact, some will almost insist you change your plans. Yes, you hire real estate professionals for their expertise. But don't allow anyone to talk you into a decision. Instead, take a bit of time to make the best choice for you. Of course, you want to stick to your timeline, but a few hours or even half a day to think it over can keep you from a mistake.

- **PLAN TO SUPERVISE THE CONTRACTORS.** Some investors allow contractors to work independently. That is usually when the investor has worked with the contractor for a long time. Even then, I have found it's better to supervise the contractor or hire someone to do so. If you don't, you may find you run overbudget, tasks aren't completed as you hope, and mix-ups occur.

> **TIP:** Make sure that the contractor obtains any needed permits for their work. Again, that is part of why you pay them.

- **TRACK THE BILLS EACH DAY, AND ALWAYS KEEP RECEIPTS.** You'll want to have them in case something needs to be returned. They're also handy to show the scope of the work you completed.

- **DON'T GET SO CAUGHT UP IN DETAILS.** Details are important, but if you forget the forest for the trees, you may not stick to the guidelines we discussed about a rapid turnover.

EXPERT ADVICE

Kyle McCormick

You may hear some experts say that it takes about 18 months to buy, renovate, and sell a property.

"Eighteen months is way too long," says McCormick who laments an approximately nine-month long project. "We did a full gut job on the first place we bought, and that is the only place we lost money on."

You may need to go a few weeks longer on your plan if you run into permit roadblocks, he adds. That's why it's important to start moving on your flip almost as soon as you buy it.

Planned Renovations: Kitchen

	PRIORITY (high, medium, or low)	ESTIMATED TIME FRAME	START DATE	BUDGET
Cabinets				
Contractor:				
Notes:				
Flooring				
Contractor:				
Notes:				
Dishwasher				
Contractor:				
Notes:				
Refrigerator				
Contractor:				
Notes:				
Stove				
Contractor:				
Notes:				

Contractor List

Company name:

Contractor name:

Contractor's phone number:

Contractor's email address:

Company mailing address:

Tasks:

Estimated time frame for work:

Hired:

Start date:

Finish date:

Invoice received (date):

Invoice paid (date):

CHAPTER 8

Staging Your Home

Your renovation is done, and now you're ready to put your house on the market. Before you put that "For Sale" sign out, you should consider staging your home. Sure, you can sell it empty. But common wisdom is that prospective buyers want to see themselves living in the house. That includes picturing how their furniture will look in the home.

Consider these facts from a 2019 National Association of Realtors report:

- Forty percent of buyers' agents cited that home staging had a positive effect on most buyers' view of the home.

- Eighty-three percent of buyers' agents said staging a home made it easier for a buyer to visualize the property as a future home.

- Staging the living room was found to be most important for buyers (47 percent), followed by staging the master bedroom (42 percent) and the kitchen (35 percent).

- One-quarter of buyers' agents said that staging a home increased the dollar value offered between 1 and 5 percent, compared to other similar homes on the market that are not staged.

Cleaning

So how do you get started? The first point of action is to clean the house. Whether you painted, added tile, or replaced carpet, dust, dirt, pieces of plaster, and debris will be everywhere. If you hired a quality contractor, they cleaned up the mess.

That's not enough.

You need to clean the house so it's showroom sparkling. Ceiling fans, baseboards, and windowpanes are among the many often-overlooked areas you must polish until they shine.

And, of course, bathrooms, kitchens, and appliances must sparkle.

Home staging isn't all about cleaning, of course.

Nicks, scratches, holes, and scuffs all draw the eyes of prospective buyers. So do doorknobs, switch plates, and even ceiling fan pulls. If you haven't already, polish or replace those.

Pull up the blinds, turn on the lights, and make the room look as airy and bright as possible.

Furnishing

Consider renting or buying secondhand furniture so that it fits the size and theme you want.

If you're staging a home for first-time homebuyers, the furniture you choose will be different from the furniture you'd choose if you were marketing to seniors. Whatever market you aim for, select smaller furniture rather than larger. You want the home to look spacious. Light-colored furniture will also make the room seem larger. Try not to buy furniture that is heavy. That way you can move it as much as needed.

Here is what NAR says are the most commonly staged rooms:

LIVING ROOM	93%
KITCHEN	84%
MASTER BEDROOM	78%

Consider these ideas for staging:

- Don't place furniture close to a wall. Instead, pull couches, tables, and chairs out. That technique is called "floating."

- Don't hang or display photographs. You never know if a photo will remind someone of a person they don't like or a bad experience.

- Use area rugs. They even look great on regular carpeting. Don't forget to put nonslip rug pads under rugs.

- Add some homey touches, such as pillows and flameless candles. Don't overdo it though. A good rule of thumb is to use three. Three throw pillows. Three flameless candles. Three pieces of furniture.

- The landscape is part of staging. Sweep the sidewalk, mow the lawn, place a welcome mat outside, and make sure the house number is easy to read.

- Add towels and a shower curtain (if appropriate) in bathrooms.

- Protect carpets. If you put new carpets in, consider buying disposable booties for prospective buyers to wear when they tour the home.

- Use window treatments. They make the home seem warmer.

- Don't forget lights. Look for floor lights and table lamps. When you stage the home, turn on the lights, even if it's sunny outside. You want the home to look as bright and light as possible.

- Appliances must shine, inside and outside. And, of course, make sure there are no crumbs or other debris in drawers or cupboards.

- Add a few placemats and a vase to a table in the kitchen or dining room. The key is to make it look homey.

Use the Home-Staging Checklist (on the next page or on page 144) to ensure you properly stage your home.

Home-Staging Checklist

- ☐ Rent furniture

- ☐ Clear clutter.
- ☐ Thoroughly clean the home.
- ☐ Have the carpets/rugs professionally cleaned.
- ☐ Clean and wax the floors.
- ☐ Clean the tops of ceiling fans.
- ☐ Touch up the paint.
- ☐ Clean windows and sills.
- ☐ Clean the floorboards.
- ☐ Set up the furniture to make the space look larger.

- ☐ Ensure toilet seats are closed.
- ☐ Hang shower curtains where appropriate.
- ☐ Ensure bulbs are high wattage.
- ☐ Turn on all lights.
- ☐ Air out rooms.
- ☐ Bake cookies or use scented sprays.
- ☐ Double-check that there are no slipping hazards.
- ☐ Invest in nonslip pads for under throw rugs.
- ☐ Set flameless candles behind fireplace screens to add elegance.
- ☐ Consider hanging a welcome sign on the door.

Remember, you don't need to treat all rooms equally. People will usually be most interested in the living and dining room. Sure, they'll likely want to know if their beds fit in the bedrooms, but you don't have to go all out there. Even a futon helps people visualize the space.

That's not to say the home should be barren. One of the nicest investment properties I ever toured had flameless candles flickering behind a lovely fireplace screen.

Of course the outside of your home needs as much TLC as possible. There's no second chance to make a great first impression. We've discussed the importance of mowed grass, trimmed bushes, and trimmed trees before. Don't forget to power wash your house, add a welcome mat, and—please—make sure your house number can be seen from the street. Few things are more annoying than trying to figure out what house is for sale because there are no numbers on the house.

It's difficult to remember everything you want to prepare before showing a house. Write a checklist so you can refer to it each time. Use the Curb Appeal Plan checklist to make sure you have curb appeal. (Find another copy of the checklist on page 144.)

Curb Appeal Plan

- ❏ Mow the lawn.
- ❏ Sweep up any leaves.
- ❏ Weed flower beds and other areas.
- ❏ Make sure all stepping stones are secure.
- ❏ Power wash the house, steps, and walkways.

- ❏ Place pots of colorful flowers outside.
- ❏ Double-check that there are no animal droppings.
- ❏ Make sure the house number is visible from the street.
- ❏ Invest in a new mailbox.
- ❏ Have the gutters cleaned.

Keep glass cleaner, paper towels, a small, handheld vacuum, a dust cloth, trash bags, and other cleaning supplies at the house. When people tour a home, they tend to drop things, track in leaves, and otherwise leave the home in less-than-perfect condition. Make sure your home sparkles each time it is shown.

> **TIP:** It's a great idea to keep a three-hole binder that shows each highlight of the home. You can use plastic binder sleeves to display brochures about appliances, carpet, and other features of the house you want to spotlight.

Trachelle Spencer

You can keep an electronic record of the work done in your home that shows the true value of property. "Automated valuation models (AVMs) such as Zillow can only capture the market trends and offer estimates on a home's value because they don't have the visibility into the interiors of the homes," says Trachelle Spencer of Lone Tree, Colorado. "If the flipper maintained electronic documentation of the renovation, the flipper could better manage their costs and ROI, but also provide peace of mind to the homebuyer. The new owner could pick up where the flipper left off. If a tile is damaged or needs to be replaced, the homebuyer could know exactly what to buy and where to buy it from. The homebuyer could even rehire the same contractor if the flipper shared the project details."

Spencer and her partner Damian Spencer founded RezDox, which she calls the CarFax of real estate, to do just that. They decided to start the company after they saw how a three-hole binder book of renovations they kept intrigued potential buyers and helped them sell their home for a higher net profit.

"We included cosmetic upgrades, granite tiling, and even the information about the contractors we used," she says. "We put the binder on the counter and people looked at it when they toured the house. We had incredible feedback."

TIP: Although you won't actively point out downsides to the home, don't hide or fib about them either. Your prospective buyers will question your honesty and avoid your home. Answer all questions honestly. Again, this is another great reason to hire a realtor. They are savvy enough to discuss such issues without risking a misunderstanding with the prospective buyer. Also, if possible, fix any problems you encounter (within reason—you won't want to put a new roof on a home that has a good year or so of life in it). Most of today's buyers want turnkey homes.

TIP: Do not plan to attend an open house. You could inadvertently do or say something to squelch interest. Allow your realtor to handle these open houses.

CHAPTER 9

For Sale

If things go as planned, just three to six months after you buy your investment property, you'll sell it. In your search for a house, you likely came across many different types of sales. There are traditional realtor-led sales. Then there are the other types I discussed earlier, including selling it yourself (for sale by owner), selling it to a wholesaler, and putting it up for auction.

If you obtained a real estate license as discussed on page 13, you may want to sell the house yourself. If not and you are a new investors, you'd do well to have a realtor sell your homes. If you've ever bought property sold by an owner, you likely know the difficulties that can arise, from errors on contracts to arguments over home inspection reports. Even though the property you renovate is not your primary residence, you will develop emotional ties to it. Smooth showings, negotiations, and closings are among the values you'll receive when you hire a realtor to represent your property. Remember, if the realtor who helped you buy your home was up front and savvy, you may want to offer the sale to them. There's no obligation, of course, but it makes sense.

The seller traditionally pays the realtor a commission. Commissions vary widely, but you'll likely find they total about 2 to 3 percent of the sale price. Don't forget, though, you can negotiate commissions too.

And, yes, you can expect to give up some control. Realtors want to sell homes as quickly as possible. That means they may not price a house as high as you'd like. A few thousand dollars extra won't significantly change their commission. Having said that, remember that even with a realtor, you are in control of the sale. Listen to the realtor, do your homework on the selling prices of like homes in the area, and then move ahead.

> **TIP:** If a realtor enjoys working with you and believes you have the potential for more quality flips, they may go the extra mile to make your sale as profitable as possible.

> **TIP:** Don't forget to display the book with all of the improvements you've made on the property. You want prospective sellers to see that book and note all of the home's quality upgrades. It will also give your realtor talking points with prospective buyers.

> **TIP:** If you're in a seller's market, getting offers will not be very difficult, which alone may undermine the cost of bringing on an agent. You will likely find offers at or even above your selling price while doing minimal leg work. It will still take work, but in a hot market, a lack of experience can be overlooked by buyer enthusiasm.

Choosing Your Realtor

On page 52, I covered some key points about how to find the agent you want to hire. Again, if you use the agent who found you this investment, you're ahead. If you didn't use an agent or don't want to work with the same one during the sale, consider these steps to choose your realtor.

- GO TO OPEN HOUSES. I've found it helpful to see how an agent presents a current house on a market. One of the first houses I bought was with a realtor I met at an open house. He was low-key, professional, and engaging. The big selling point, though, was that he clearly understood the houses in the neighborhood in which I wanted to buy. Why wouldn't I use him to help me find a house?

- **CHOOSE SOMEONE WHO HAS SOLD FLIPPED HOUSES.** You'll have an advantage if your realtor has sold investment houses before. It's not mandatory, of course. But there are certain selling points for flipped homes that realtors who don't work with them might not know. Realtors who sell investment properties can explain why your house is superior to other similarly valued houses in the area. Plus, a realtor who works with flipped houses won't put your presumably lower-priced home on the back burner and concentrate on other sales.

- **READ THE CONTRACT FOR EARLY EXIT FEES.** I can't stress this highly enough. When you are signing with a realtor, everyone is happy and excited. If a week or two into the project you find that the realtor isn't doing what you expected, you may be stuck unless you pay a penalty. Don't be shy about shopping around for a realtor. I would have saved myself many headaches if I had done that on my last sale.

- **SET CLEAR EXPECTATIONS.** Try to temper your enthusiasm and take your lifestyle and needs into consideration. Are you comfortable with open houses being held at the property? If so, will your realtor be in attendance or will it be someone from the realtor's office? Do you mind a lockbox on the property so realtors can show prospective clients the home when no one else is there? How will the realtor follow up with others whose clients toured your property? These are just some of the questions you should ask *before* you sign the contract.

- **DO YOUR DUE DILIGENCE.** How many properties have they sold? How many listings do they currently have? How big is their team? Do as much research as you can and always check references. Once you find a good realtor, you can use them again and again, so invest the time up front.

The Offer

If things go as you hope, you will quickly receive an offer, or perhaps several. One of the greatest benefits of working with a realtor is that they understand the intricacies of offers and can help you decide which ones to pass on or the best one to accept. Again, the decision is yours, but listen to your realtor's guidance. After all, they want to sell the property too.

Unless you have an all-cash, no-contingency offer—which is quite rare—you will likely encounter several pros and cons in the offers. It's important to pay attention to those because they can slow down and even halt the buying process. That's especially true if the buyer has not made a home purchase before.

That's not to say you should avoid first-time homebuyers. It's just important to remember they are often not aware of the complexities of real estate sales, so may make some stumbles that delay the process. Patience is key.

Here are some of the points you may encounter when you review offers:

- **ARE THERE CONTINGENCIES?** Contingencies mean that the buyer agrees to the sale, but only if something else occurs first. Perhaps the most common "contingency" is one in which the buyer must first sell their property. That is often undesirable today. One reason is that you have no knowledge of the property they need to sell, or its market. Such a contingency usually equals a pass.

- **ARE THE POTENTIAL BUYERS ABLE TO PAY FOR THE HOUSE?** Many buyers are preapproved for a certain amount of financing. Your realtor will know what proof is needed to ensure that the preapproval is legitimate.

- **WHAT IS THE HOME INSPECTION CONTINGENCY?** Make sure that a licensed inspector is hired. Find out the name of the inspector and the date and time of the inspection.

- **WHAT EARNEST MONEY IS OFFERED?** As you likely know, earnest money proves a buyer's commitment to the purchase of your property. If the buyer cancels the purchase, the earnest money is yours to keep. Consider how much would compensate you if you got within days of a closing and the buyer decided not to proceed.

Robyn Porter, a Washington, DC, area realtor, tells *Realtor Magazine* that she urges her clients to offer enough earnest money to "stand out." If a client makes an offer on a $500,000 home, she suggests a $20,000 or $25,000 earnest money deposit to catch the sellers' attention and prove they are serious about the purchase.

Track and analyze your offers on a worksheet like the following (see page 146 for a Weighing the Offers worksheet you can use).

Weighing the Offers

Date:		Deadline to respond to seller:	
Buyer:		Contact information:	
Agent/representative:		Contact information:	
Offer:	Earnest money:	Loan amount:	Cash:
Qualified buyer?	Inspection:	Appraisal:	Survey of the land:
Contingencies:			
Closing date:	Move-in date:	Rent-back option?	

Ensuring the Home Has No Major Faults

Many realtors urge their clients to buy a home contingent on a home inspection. There's no reason to avoid a home inspection. No home, not even a new build, is ever perfect. If you've hired an agent, they will likely prepare you for what to expect and how you can help the inspection go smoothly.

Use the Prepare for the Buyer's Home Inspection checklist on the following page or on page 149 to prepare for your buyer's home inspection.

Prepare for the Buyer's Home Inspection

- ❏ Turn HVAC on and off to ensure it works properly.
- ❏ Replace all HVAC filters.
- ❏ Clean stove, oven, microwave, refrigerator, dishwasher.
- ❏ Ensure access to attic and basement.
- ❏ Open and close all windows.
- ❏ Ensure all toilets, showers, and water faucets work.
- ❏ Test smoke detectors.
- ❏ Test all electrical outlets.
- ❏ Ensure ceiling fans work.

- ❏ Open and close the garage door (manually and with an automatic closer).
- ❏ Make sure all screens are in good order.
- ❏ Make sure downspouts are not clogged.
- ❏ Double-check for rodents or pest activity.
- ❏ Ensure no tree limbs hang over the roof.
- ❏ Make sure the gutters are clear.
- ❏ Spot-check the roof for missing shingles.

Consider these points prior to the inspection report:

- **CONSIDER A PRE-INSPECTION.** This is rarely needed, but if you are nervous about the home inspection, ask your realtor to arrange a pre-inspection. That will allow you to get ahead of any problems that might be cited when the buyer's inspector reviews the house.

- **KEEP YOUR HOUSE CLEAN AND TIDY EVERY DAY.** If you start to let the appearance of the house slip, it creates a poor impression. The buyer wants to know that they made a good decision. Don't give them any overt reason to believe otherwise.

- **REALIZE A HOME INSPECTOR WILL LIKELY FIND DEFICIENCIES.** Again, no home is perfect. If you've followed the plan to rehab your home and used contractors, there should not be major surprises. But there is no guarantee there won't be. When I bought my last house, the home inspector discovered that the one-year-old hot water heater was improperly installed. I would have accepted repair credits from the seller, but they opted to have it replaced.

- **DO NOT ATTEND THE HOME INSPECTION.** The prospective buyer, the inspector, and the inspector's realtor will attend. Your realtor may attend. Make sure you don't.

- **MAJOR VS. MINOR FIXES.** If you are selling in a hot market or neighborhood, your realtor and the buyer may agree that you needn't fix minor issues such as a loose gutter. Expect to fix any health or safety issues, of course.

- **LEAVE ALL UTILITIES ON.** This sounds like a no-brainer, but in an effort to save money, some home sellers will turn off utilities to save money. Doing so can ruin pipes, which can serve as an entryway for pests.

- **DO NOT ATTEND THE HOME INSPECTION.** The prospective buyer, the inspector, and the inspector's realtor will attend. Your realtor may attend. Make sure you don't.

- **BE FLEXIBLE.** Yes, you want to know the time and day of the inspection. We all know babysitters don't arrive on time, a dog runs away, or a work meeting drones on. Your prospective buyer will appreciate your understanding if the home inspection does not take place exactly as scheduled.

The Closing

If things go as planned, the days before the closing will come off smoothly. Your realtor is likely in touch with the prospective buyer's realtor so can alert you to any bumps. Still, there may be a few surprises during the closing. Although the following issues aren't common, it's still important to know they may happen.

- **FINANCING FALLS THROUGH.** If a potential buyer experiences a major change in their finances—such as job loss or even sudden, major credit card debt—between the time you accept the offer and the time you close, it could impact their ability to receive a loan. Another problem may be that the lender could not verify some of the information on the buyer's application. Lenders always double-check a loan application before a purchase is finalized.

- **THE APPRAISAL IS LOW.** Lenders require property appraisals before finalizing a loan. If the appraisal of your property is low, financing may be withdrawn. Your realtor can advise you on a solution. It could include lowering your asking price or asking the prospective buyer to pay cash for the difference.

- **LIENS ON YOUR PROPERTY.** If you followed the advice from Chapter 4 of this book, you conducted a title search of the property before you bought it. Still, unpaid taxes or a contractor's unpaid fees are just some of the reasons your home could have a lien on it. Your realtor and the buyer's realtor can negotiate how to clear those liens.

- **SOMEONE BACKS OUT.** The most common scenario is that the buyer decides not to move ahead with the sale. In that case, you keep the earnest money. IMPORTANT: Do not cancel the sale without a lot of thought and discussion. Your potential buyer and your agent can both sue you.

CHAPTER 10

Frequently Asked Questions

No book can cover every aspect of home flipping and selling. Every situation is different. Those that begin their home-flipping journeys often have similar questions. Although most of these topics are covered in the book, this question-and-answer section will help you easily find the answer to common queries.

Q: Do I have to have a lot of money to begin to flip homes?

A: No. This book mentions several investors who started with very little up-front capital when they began to flip homes. There is no one answer about how much money you need to flip a house. That's because there are too many variables. Investors agree that good credit and a purchase that does not put your current lifestyle at stake are important factors.

Q: Why do I need to join an investors' group?

A: No one forces you to join an investors' group, but most savvy home flippers started out in one. Flipping real estate is complicated. The best way to learn the nuances is through other investors. Most investors say their colleagues are very forthcoming about opportunities and challenges.

Most groups are free. And the networking is invaluable. Groups help others find optimal properties, find high-quality contractors, avoid scams, and more. The question should really be why wouldn't you join an investors' group? Find one online at BiggerPockets.com and MeetUp.

Q: I've read no real "skills" are needed before you flip a home. Is that true?

A: In a way. You don't need to be a realtor, a contractor, or another type of real estate professional to make home flipping work. If there is one quality you need, it's motivation. Home flipping is a relatively long and costly journey. If you are motivated to learn about it; put in the time, effort, and cash to successfully flip a home; and learn how to sell for a profit, your ultimate reward could be a new career or lucrative second income.

One of the most important criteria is to be honest with yourself. If you dread learning about real estate, have many hobbies or interests that will pull your attention away from the project, or are in a precarious financial situation, this is likely not the time to try home flipping.

Q: Why is it important to flip a house quickly? Can't I take my time?

A: Not if you want to earn a profit on the house. Are there exceptions to this rule? Yes. But even three months is a long time to spend flipping a house. Markets change quickly. And if you have a loan for your home or renovations—whether private or from a traditional lender—the longer you take the more interest you must pay. The goal in successful home flipping is to get in and out fast.

Q: How do I know how much money I will need for the renovation?

A: The best way to estimate costs is to assemble a team for your project. Realtors, landscapers, contractors, and even handymen can give you estimates about what work needs to be done and the cost of labor and supplies. That's why I urge you to assemble a team before you fully commit to buying a home. And the real estate investors' group I mentioned will also offer you plentiful information about what homes and renovations offer the most promise for quick, lucrative sales. Still, no one truly knows how much a project will cost until the work begins. Unsafe wiring, plumbing issues, and structural concerns may all pop up in the course of the project. That's one reason realtors rarely allow a client to buy a property until a home inspection is completed.

Q: Should I hire a mentor to get me started?

A: Most real estate investors say no, not in the beginning. There are plenty of free resources you can tap into to educate yourself about home flipping. Your first flips will also teach you a lot about the journey. If you decide to become a full-time real estate flipper and need one-on-one advice for certain homes, markets, or expansions, you may consider a mentor. But you shouldn't do that until you have exhausted the abundant free information that is available.

Q: Do I need to start a business that specializes in flipping houses?

A: That depends on many variables. You likely do not need to do so, though you may pay higher taxes if you flip homes without doing so. Talk to other investors in your area and your realtor for initial guidance.

Q: Should I get a real estate license before I begin to flip houses?

A: There's no requirement to do so, but many people find it is helpful. Realtors know all the ins and outs of buying properties, renovating them, and selling them for a net profit. They also have access to property listings that many outside the industry do not. Another reason to consider pursuing a realtor's license: as you learn the business, you may find that you don't enjoy the prospect of flipping houses as much as you initially thought you would. It's better to find that out before you purchase a home.

Q: What is the most important part of home flipping?

A: The amount of money you pay for the home. The saying that you make the money when you buy, not when you sell, is true. Initially, you want to buy a rough diamond that doesn't need a lot to of polishing before potential buyers recognize it's a jewel. And you don't want to buy that house for more than 70 percent of the After Repair Value (ARV) of the home.

Q: How do I calculate the ARV?

A: This is where first-time home flippers can benefit from the expertise of a real estate professional. The key is to estimate how much the property can sell for once all needed repairs are made.

When you estimate the property's likely asking price, multiply that by 0.7. That is the maximum amount of money you should spend on the house.

Q: If I only pay 70 percent of the ARV for the house and renovation, why aren't my net profits 30 percent?

A: Many variables go into flipping a house. You never know if a minor repair will become major, once budget-friendly supplies jump in price or the market begins to decline. The 70 percent rule is devised to keep you from losing money on a flip.

Q: Is there a common failing associated with new home flippers?

A: Yes, not having an exit strategy. Again, that's where other investors and your realtor can help you. If the market begins to fall or a negative is discovered—such as a high-profile crime in the neighborhood or a natural disaster nearby—you want to be able to get out of the property quickly with as little financial loss as possible. The same is true if you lose your job or develop a health issue. Plan an exit strategy for each step of your project.

Conclusion

There are many different styles of home flipping. The most successful ones are those in which the seller analyzes their goals, calculates their finances, plans their renovations, and works the plan.

Use this journal as a living document to follow your plans to the finish line.

Worksheet Appendix

The appendix contains the worksheets you may be using over and over again, reorganized into these categories: 1) finances, 2) looking for a house, 3) renovating the house, and 4) selling the house.

Do the Math to Meet Your Goal

	AMOUNT
1. Future sale of the house	
2. Divide the amount by 1.20 (for a 20 percent profit).	
3. Determine the cost of repairs and renovations.	
4. Analyze other costs: Real estate agent fees	
Closing costs	
Property taxes (6 months)	
HOA fees (6 months)	
5. Maximum price to pay for the house	

Estimated Repair Costs: Landscaping

Project:	Budget:

Details:

Contractor:	Contact information:

Notes:

Project:	Budget:

Details:

Contractor:	Contact information:

Notes:

Project:	Budget:

Details:

Contractor:	Contact information:

Notes:

Estimated Repair Costs: Landscaping

Project: | Budget:

Details:

Contractor: | Contact information:

Notes:

Project: | Budget:

Details:

Contractor: | Contact information:

Notes:

Project: | Budget:

Details:

Contractor: | Contact information:

Notes:

Estimated Repair Costs: Landscaping

Project: | Budget:

Details:

Contractor: | Contact information:

Notes:

Project: | Budget:

Details:

Contractor: | Contact information:

Notes:

Project: | Budget:

Details:

Contractor: | Contact information:

Notes:

Estimated Repair Costs: Landscaping

Project: | Budget:

Details:

Contractor: | Contact information:

Notes:

Project: | Budget:

Details:

Contractor: | Contact information:

Notes:

Project: | Budget:

Details:

Contractor: | Contact information:

Notes:

Estimated Repair Costs: Home Exterior

Project: | Budget:

Details:

Contractor: | Contact information:

Notes:

Project: | Budget:

Details:

Contractor: | Contact information:

Notes:

Project: | Budget:

Details:

Contractor: | Contact information:

Notes:

Estimated Repair Costs: Home Exterior

Project: | Budget:

Details:

Contractor: | Contact information:

Notes:

Project: | Budget:

Details:

Contractor: | Contact information:

Notes:

Project: | Budget:

Details:

Contractor: | Contact information:

Notes:

Estimated Repair Costs: Home Exterior

Project: Budget:

Details:

Contractor: Contact information:

Notes:

Project: Budget:

Details:

Contractor: Contact information:

Notes:

Project: Budget:

Details:

Contractor: Contact information:

Notes:

Estimated Repair Costs: Home Exterior

Project: | Budget:

Details:

Contractor: | Contact information:

Notes:

Project: | Budget:

Details:

Contractor: | Contact information:

Notes:

Project: | Budget:

Details:

Contractor: | Contact information:

Notes:

Estimated Repair Costs: Home Interior

Project: | Budget:

Details:

Contractor: | Contact information:

Notes:

Project: | Budget:

Details:

Contractor: | Contact information:

Notes:

Project: | Budget:

Details:

Contractor: | Contact information:

Notes:

Estimated Repair Costs: Home Interior

Project: | Budget:

Details:

Contractor: | Contact information:

Notes:

Project: | Budget:

Details:

Contractor: | Contact information:

Notes:

Project: | Budget:

Details:

Contractor: | Contact information:

Notes:

Estimated Repair Costs: Home Interior

Project: | Budget:

Details:

Contractor: | Contact information:

Notes:

Project: | Budget:

Details:

Contractor: | Contact information:

Notes:

Project: | Budget:

Details:

Contractor: | Contact information:

Notes:

Estimated Repair Costs: Home Interior

Project:	Budget:

Details:

Contractor:	Contact information:

Notes:

Project:	Budget:

Details:

Contractor:	Contact information:

Notes:

Project:	Budget:

Details:

Contractor:	Contact information:

Notes:

Estimated Repair Costs: Additional Projects

Project: | Budget:

Details:

Contractor: | Contact information:

Notes:

Project: | Budget:

Details:

Contractor: | Contact information:

Notes:

Project: | Budget:

Details:

Contractor: | Contact information:

Notes:

Estimated Repair Costs: Additional Projects

Project: | Budget:

Details:

Contractor: | Contact information:

Notes:

Project: | Budget:

Details:

Contractor: | Contact information:

Notes:

Project: | Budget:

Details:

Contractor: | Contact information:

Notes:

Estimated Repair Costs: Additional Projects

Project: | Budget:

Details:

Contractor: | Contact information:

Notes:

Project: | Budget:

Details:

Contractor: | Contact information:

Notes:

Project: | Budget:

Details:

Contractor: | Contact information:

Notes:

Estimated Repair Costs: Additional Projects

Project: | Budget:

Details:

Contractor: | Contact information:

Notes:

Project: | Budget:

Details:

Contractor: | Contact information:

Notes:

Project: | Budget:

Details:

Contractor: | Contact information:

Notes:

Total Budget

	AMOUNT
Estimated purchase price (see Do The Math to Meet Your Goal, page 10):	
Estimated fees (see Do The Math to Meet Your Goal, page 10):	
Estimated repair costs — Landscaping:	
Home exterior:	
Home interior:	
Additional projects:	
Total:	

Financing Your Home

Liquid savings	Company:	Estimated amount:	Contact information:
	Notes:		

Refinancing primary home	Company:	Estimated amount:	Contact information:
	Notes:		

Home equity loan	Company:	Estimated amount:	Contact information:
	Notes:		

Home equity financing	Company:	Estimated amount:	Contact information:
	Notes:		

Home equity line of credit	Company:	Estimated amount:	Contact information:
	Notes:		

Reverse mortgage	Company:	Estimated amount:	Contact information:
	Notes:		

Private money lenders	Company:	Estimated amount:	Contact information:
	Notes:		

Traditional bank loan	Company:	Estimated amount:	Contact information:
	Notes:		

Taking on other investors	Company:	Estimated amount:	Contact information:
	Notes:		

Hard money lenders	Company:	Estimated amount:	Contact information:
	Notes:		

Financing Your Home

Liquid savings	Company:	Estimated amount:	Contact information:
	Notes:		

Refinancing primary home	Company:	Estimated amount:	Contact information:
	Notes:		

Home equity loan	Company:	Estimated amount:	Contact information:
	Notes:		

Home equity financing	Company:	Estimated amount:	Contact information:
	Notes:		

Home equity line of credit	Company:	Estimated amount:	Contact information:
	Notes:		

Reverse mortgage	Company:	Estimated amount:	Contact information:
	Notes:		

Private money lenders	Company:	Estimated amount:	Contact information:
	Notes:		

Traditional bank loan	Company:	Estimated amount:	Contact information:
	Notes:		

Taking on other investors	Company:	Estimated amount:	Contact information:
	Notes:		

Hard money lenders	Company:	Estimated amount:	Contact information:
	Notes:		

Possible Private Money Lenders

TOTAL AMOUNT NEEDED:

Possible partner:	Phone/email:
Loan amount:	Interest rate:

Loan terms:

Date contacted/notes:

Possible partner:	Phone/email:
Loan amount:	Interest rate:

Loan terms:

Date contacted/notes:

Possible partner:	Phone/email:
Loan amount:	Interest rate:

Loan terms:

Date contacted/notes:

Traditional Lenders

Bank name:

Contact name: | Phone/email:

Loan amount: | Interest rate:

Loan terms:

Notes:

Bank name:

Contact name: | Phone/email:

Loan amount: | Interest rate:

Loan terms:

Notes:

Bank name:

Contact name: | Phone/email:

Loan amount: | Interest rate:

Loan terms:

Notes:

Daily Expense Form

Date:	Purchase:	Cost:	Category:

Notes:

Date:	Purchase:	Cost:	Category:

Notes:

Date:	Purchase:	Cost:	Category:

Notes:

Date:	Purchase:	Cost:	Category:

Notes:

Date:	Purchase:	Cost:	Category:

Notes:

Date:	Purchase:	Cost:	Category:

Notes:

Homes to Consider

Address:

List price:	Estimated renovation cost:	Expected net income:
Realtor/owner:	Contact information:	

Notes:

Address:

List price:	Estimated renovation cost:	Expected net income:
Realtor/owner:	Contact information:	

Notes:

Address:

List price:	Estimated renovation cost:	Expected net income:
Realtor/owner:	Contact information:	

Notes:

Possible Home Inspectors

Name:	Phone/email:
Company name:	Address:
Fee:	Availability:

Notes:

Name:	Phone/email:
Company name:	Address:
Fee:	Availability:

Notes:

Name:	Phone/email:
Company name:	Address:
Fee:	Availability:

Notes:

Possible Home Inspectors

Name: | Phone/email:

Company name: | Address:

Fee: | Availability:

Notes:

Name: | Phone/email:

Company name: | Address:

Fee: | Availability:

Notes:

Name: | Phone/email:

Company name: | Address:

Fee: | Availability:

Notes:

Possible Home Inspectors

Name:

Phone/email:

Company name:

Address:

Fee:

Availability:

Notes:

Name:

Phone/email:

Company name:

Address:

Fee:

Availability:

Notes:

Name:

Phone/email:

Company name:

Address:

Fee:

Availability:

Notes:

Competition Log

HOMES THAT SOLD QUICKLY

Address:

List price:	Sales price:	Days on the market:

Notes:

HOMES THAT ARE STUCK ON THE MARKET

Address:

List price:	Sales price:	Days on the market:

Notes:

HOMES UNDER CONTRACT

Address:

List price:	Sales price:	Days on the market:

Notes:

Competition Log

HOMES THAT SOLD QUICKLY

Address:

List price:	Sales price:	Days on the market:

Notes:

HOMES THAT ARE STUCK ON THE MARKET

Address:

List price:	Sales price:	Days on the market:

Notes:

HOMES UNDER CONTRACT

Address:

List price:	Sales price:	Days on the market:

Notes:

Competition Log

HOMES THAT SOLD QUICKLY

Address:

List price:	Sales price:	Days on the market:

Notes:

HOMES THAT ARE STUCK ON THE MARKET

Address:

List price:	Sales price:	Days on the market:

Notes:

HOMES UNDER CONTRACT

Address:

List price:	Sales price:	Days on the market:

Notes:

Areas for Consideration

Area name:

Median income: | Median age: | Crime rate:

Livability score: | School ratings:

Notes:

Area name:

Median income: | Median age: | Crime rate:

Livability score: | School ratings:

Notes:

Area name:

Median income: | Median age: | Crime rate:

Livability score: | School ratings:

Notes:

Area name:

Median income: | Median age: | Crime rate:

Livability score: | School ratings:

Notes:

Realtor Information

Realtor's name	Company	Phone	Email	Additional notes

Assessing Contractors

Name:

Company name:

Specialty:

Contact information:

Was the contractor on time?

Does the contractor return calls and messages?

Does the contractor have the right tools and knowledge?

Was the estimate accurate?

Did the contractor conduct follow-up checks?

Notes:

Name:

Company name:

Specialty:

Contact information:

Was the contractor on time?

Does the contractor return calls and messages?

Does the contractor have the right tools and knowledge?

Was the estimate accurate?

Did the contractor conduct follow-up checks?

Notes:

Assessing Contractors

Name:	Company name:

Specialty:

Contact information:

Was the contractor on time?	Does the contractor return calls and messages?

Does the contractor have the right tools and knowledge?

Was the estimate accurate?	Did the contractor conduct follow-up checks?

Notes:

Name:	Company name:

Specialty:

Contact information:

Was the contractor on time?	Does the contractor return calls and messages?

Does the contractor have the right tools and knowledge?

Was the estimate accurate?	Did the contractor conduct follow-up checks?

Notes:

Possible Properties

Address:

Asking price:	Realtor/owner:	Contact information:

Notes:

Address:

Asking price:	Realtor/owner:	Contact information:

Notes:

Address:

Asking price:	Realtor/owner:	Contact information:

Notes:

Address:

Asking price:	Realtor/owner:	Contact information:

Notes:

Address:

Asking price:	Realtor/owner:	Contact information:

Notes:

Home Inspection Information

Inspector name: | Contact information:

EXTERIOR

Roof: | Gutters:

Other areas:

INTERIOR

Appliances: | HVAC: | Hot water heater:

Other areas:

OTHER QUESTIONS/NOTES

Statement of Work (SOW)

Company name: | Contractor name:

Contractor's phone number: | Contractor's email address:

Company mailing address:

Project:

Description: | Due date:

Products needed	Brand	Cost	Delivery date
1			
2			
3			
4			
		Total cost:	

Project:

Description: | Due date:

Products needed	Brand	Cost	Delivery date
1			
2			
3			
4			
		Total cost:	

Additional contractor fees:

Expenses:			
1			
2			
3			
Mileage/travel:			
1			
2			
3			
Contract modifications:			
Project	Modification		
1			
2			
3			
Termination date:			

Planned Renovations: Kitchen

	PRIORITY (high, medium, or low)	ESTIMATED TIME FRAME	START DATE	BUDGET
Contractor:				
Notes:				
Contractor:				
Notes:				
Contractor:				
Notes:				
Contractor:				
Notes:				
Contractor:				
Notes:				

Planned Renovations: Bathroom

	PRIORITY (high, medium, or low)	ESTIMATED TIME FRAME	START DATE	BUDGET
Contractor:				
Notes:				
Contractor:				
Notes:				
Contractor:				
Notes:				
Contractor:				
Notes:				
Contractor:				
Notes:				

Planned Renovations: Bathroom

	PRIORITY (high, medium, or low)	ESTIMATED TIME FRAME	START DATE	BUDGET
Contractor:				
Notes:				
Contractor:				
Notes:				
Contractor:				
Notes:				
Contractor:				
Notes:				
Contractor:				
Notes:				

Planned Renovations: Bedroom

	PRIORITY (high, medium, or low)	ESTIMATED TIME FRAME	START DATE	BUDGET
	Contractor:			
	Notes:			
	Contractor:			
	Notes:			
	Contractor:			
	Notes:			
	Contractor:			
	Notes:			
	Contractor:			
	Notes:			

Planned Renovations: Bedroom

	PRIORITY (high, medium, or low)	ESTIMATED TIME FRAME	START DATE	BUDGET
Contractor:				
Notes:				
Contractor:				
Notes:				
Contractor:				
Notes:				
Contractor:				
Notes:				
Contractor:				
Notes:				

Planned Renovations: Bedroom

	PRIORITY (high, medium, or low)	ESTIMATED TIME FRAME	START DATE	BUDGET
Contractor:				
Notes:				
Contractor:				
Notes:				
Contractor:				
Notes:				
Contractor:				
Notes:				
Contractor:				
Notes:				

Planned Renovations: Living Room

	PRIORITY (high, medium, or low)	ESTIMATED TIME FRAME	START DATE	BUDGET
Contractor:				
Notes:				
Contractor:				
Notes:				
Contractor:				
Notes:				
Contractor:				
Notes:				
Contractor:				
Notes:				

Planned Renovations: Dining Room

	PRIORITY (high, medium, or low)	ESTIMATED TIME FRAME	START DATE	BUDGET
	Contractor:			
	Notes:			
	Contractor:			
	Notes:			
	Contractor:			
	Notes:			
	Contractor:			
	Notes:			
	Contractor:			
	Notes:			

Planned Renovations: Electrical Work

	PRIORITY (high, medium, or low)	ESTIMATED TIME FRAME	START DATE	BUDGET
Contractor:				
Notes:				
Contractor:				
Notes:				
Contractor:				
Notes:				
Contractor:				
Notes:				
Contractor:				
Notes:				

Planned Renovations: Painting

	PRIORITY (high, medium, or low)	ESTIMATED TIME FRAME	START DATE	BUDGET
Contractor:				
Notes:				
Contractor:				
Notes:				
Contractor:				
Notes:				
Contractor:				
Notes:				
Contractor:				
Notes:				

Planned Renovations:

	PRIORITY (high, medium, or low)	ESTIMATED TIME FRAME	START DATE	BUDGET
Contractor:				
Notes:				
Contractor:				
Notes:				
Contractor:				
Notes:				
Contractor:				
Notes:				
Contractor:				
Notes:				

Planned Renovations:

	PRIORITY (high, medium, or low)	ESTIMATED TIME FRAME	START DATE	BUDGET
	Contractor:			
	Notes:			
	Contractor:			
	Notes:			
	Contractor:			
	Notes:			
	Contractor:			
	Notes:			
	Contractor:			
	Notes:			

Planned Renovations:

	PRIORITY (high, medium, or low)	ESTIMATED TIME FRAME	START DATE	BUDGET
Contractor:				
Notes:				
Contractor:				
Notes:				
Contractor:				
Notes:				
Contractor:				
Notes:				
Contractor:				
Notes:				

Contractor List

Company name:

Contractor name:

Contractor's phone number:

Contractor's email address:

Company mailing address:

Tasks:

Estimated time frame for work:

Hired:

Start date:

Finish date:

Invoice received (date):

Invoice paid (date):

Company name:

Contractor name:

Contractor's phone number:

Contractor's email address:

Company mailing address:

Tasks:

Estimated time frame for work:

Hired:

Start date:

Finish date:

Invoice received (date):

Invoice paid (date):

Company name:

Contractor name:

Contractor's phone number:

Contractor's email address:

Company mailing address:

Tasks:

Estimated time frame for work:

Hired:

Start date:

Finish date:

Invoice received (date):

Invoice paid (date):

Contractor List

Company name:

Contractor name:

Contractor's phone number:

Contractor's email address:

Company mailing address:

Tasks:

Estimated time frame for work:

Hired:

Start date:

Finish date:

Invoice received (date):

Invoice paid (date):

Company name:

Contractor name:

Contractor's phone number:

Contractor's email address:

Company mailing address:

Tasks:

Estimated time frame for work:

Hired:

Start date:

Finish date:

Invoice received (date):

Invoice paid (date):

Company name:

Contractor name:

Contractor's phone number:

Contractor's email address:

Company mailing address:

Tasks:

Estimated time frame for work:

Hired:

Start date:

Finish date:

Invoice received (date):

Invoice paid (date):

Home-Staging Checklist

❑ Rent furniture

❑ Clear clutter.

❑ Thoroughly clean the home.

❑ Have the carpets/rugs professionally cleaned.

❑ Clean and wax the floors.

❑ Clean the tops of ceiling fans.

❑ Touch up the paint.

❑ Clean windows and sills.

❑ Clean the floorboards.

❑ Set up the furniture to make the space look larger.

❑ Ensure toilet seats are closed.

❑ Hang shower curtains where appropriate.

❑ Ensure bulbs are high wattage.

❑ Turn on all lights.

❑ Air out rooms.

❑ Bake cookies or use scented sprays.

❑ Double-check that there are no slipping hazards.

❑ Invest in nonslip pads for under throw rugs.

❑ Set flameless candles behind fireplace screens to add elegance.

❑ Consider hanging a welcome sign on the door.

Curb Appeal Plan

❑ Mow the lawn.

❑ Sweep up any leaves.

❑ Weed flower beds and other areas.

❑ Make sure all stepping stones are secure.

❑ Power wash the house, steps, and walkways.

❑ Place pots of colorful flowers outside.

❑ Double-check that there are no animal droppings.

❑ Make sure the house number is visible from the street.

❑ Invest in a new mailbox.

❑ Have the gutters cleaned.

Weighing the Offers

Date:		Deadline to respond to seller:	
Buyer:		Contact information:	
Agent/representative:		Contact information:	
Offer:	Earnest money:	Loan amount:	Cash:
Qualified buyer?	Inspection:	Appraisal:	Survey of the land:
Contingencies:			
Closing date:	Move-in date:	Rent-back option?	

Date:		Deadline to respond to seller:	
Buyer:		Contact information:	
Agent/representative:		Contact information:	
Offer:	Earnest money:	Loan amount:	Cash:
Qualified buyer?	Inspection:	Appraisal:	Survey of the land:
Contingencies:			
Closing date:	Move-in date:	Rent-back option?	

Weighing the Offers

Date:		Deadline to respond to seller:	
Buyer:		Contact information:	
Agent/representative:		Contact information:	

Offer:	Earnest money:	Loan amount:	Cash:
Qualified buyer?	Inspection:	Appraisal:	Survey of the land:

Contingencies:

Closing date:	Move-in date:	Rent-back option?

Date:		Deadline to respond to seller:	
Buyer:		Contact information:	
Agent/representative:		Contact information:	

Offer:	Earnest money:	Loan amount:	Cash:
Qualified buyer?	Inspection:	Appraisal:	Survey of the land:

Contingencies:

Closing date:	Move-in date:	Rent-back option?

Weighing the Offers

Date:		Deadline to respond to seller:	
Buyer:		Contact information:	
Agent/representative:		Contact information:	
Offer:	Earnest money:	Loan amount:	Cash:
Qualified buyer?	Inspection:	Appraisal:	Survey of the land:
Contingencies:			
Closing date:	Move-in date:	Rent-back option?	

Date:		Deadline to respond to seller:	
Buyer:		Contact information:	
Agent/representative:		Contact information:	
Offer:	Earnest money:	Loan amount:	Cash:
Qualified buyer?	Inspection:	Appraisal:	Survey of the land:
Contingencies:			
Closing date:	Move-in date:	Rent-back option?	

Weighing the Offers

Date:	Deadline to respond to seller:

Buyer:	Contact information:

Agent/representative:	Contact information:

Offer:	Earnest money:	Loan amount:	Cash:

Qualified buyer?	Inspection:	Appraisal:	Survey of the land:

Contingencies:

Closing date:	Move-in date:	Rent-back option?

Date:	Deadline to respond to seller:

Buyer:	Contact information:

Agent/representative:	Contact information:

Offer:	Earnest money:	Loan amount:	Cash:

Qualified buyer?	Inspection:	Appraisal:	Survey of the land:

Contingencies:

Closing date:	Move-in date:	Rent-back option?

Prepare for the Buyer's Home Inspection

Date of Inspection:

❑ Turn HVAC on and off to ensure it works properly.

❑ Replace all HVAC filters.

❑ Clean stove, oven, microwave, refrigerator, dishwasher.

❑ Ensure access to attic and basement.

❑ Open and close all windows.

❑ Ensure all toilets, showers, and water faucets work.

❑ Test smoke detectors.

❑ Test all electrical outlets.

❑ Ensure ceiling fans work.

❑ Open and close the garage door (manually and with an automatic closer).

❑ Check all screens are in good order.

❑ Make sure downspouts are not clogged.

❑ Double-check for rodents or pest activity.

❑ Ensure no tree limbs hang over the roof.

❑ Make sure the gutters are clear.

❑ Spot check the roof for missing shingles.

About the Author

Nancy Dunham is a former staff editor with Bob Vila and has written about real estate, home improvement, and home flipping for *USA Today*, *Weichert*, *Costco Connection*, and other publications. Her work also appears in *AARP*, *The New York Times*, and *The Washington Post*.